HUMOUR IN THE LIVES OF GREAT MEN

About the Author

Jagdish Chandra Sharma received his Master's Degrees in Political Science and English in 1953 and 1955, respectively, from Punjab University, Chandigarh.

He served as a lecturer in Political Science at Guru Ram Rai College, Nahan (H.P.) (now Government College) from 1956 to 1962. He was Head of the Political Science Department at D.A.V. College, Ambala from 1963 to 1968; Head of the Post-Graduate Department of Political Science at Dayanand (Evening) College, Hissar, from 1968 to 1972; Principal, Mewat Degree College, Nagina, (now Government College) from 1972 to 1975; and Assistant Chief Editor, Section, Encyclopaedia of Indian Literature, National Sahitya Academy from 1975 to 1979.

He has to his credit a number of books, including "*Gandhi the Humanist*" (1964); "*Nehru the Humanist*" (1965); "*The Political Philosophy of Jawaharlal Nehru*" (1966) and "*Indian Prime Ministership*" (2002) and "Poetic Musings" in 2004. He also contributed from time to time, to *Caravan*, the *Illustrated Weekly* and the *Organizer*.

Humour in the Lives of Great Men

Dr. Jagdish Chandra Sharma

CONCEPT PUBLISHING COMPANY PVT. LTD.,
NEW DELHI-110059

ISBN-13: 978-81-8069-566-7

First Published 1994

Third Edition 2011

Published and Printed by

Concept Since 1974

Concept Publishing Company Pvt. Ltd.

Regd. Office:

A/15-16, Commercial Block, Mohan Garden,
New Delhi-110059 (INDIA)
Phones : 25351460, 25351794, *Fax* : 091-11-25357109
Email : publishing@conceptpub.com,
Website: www.conceptpub.com

Editorial Office:

H-13, Bali Nagar, New Delhi-110 015, India.

Cataloging in Publication Data--*Courtesy:* D.K. Agencies (P) Ltd. <docinfo@dkagencies.com>

Sharma, Jagdish Chandra, 1928-
Humour in the lives of great men / Jagdish Chandra Sharma.
p. cm.
Includes index.
ISBN 9788180695667

1. Celebrities--Anecdotes. 2. Nationalists--India--Anecdotes. 3. History, Modern--Anecdotes. I. Title.

DDC 920.02 22

Dedicated

To

Late Shri Bhagwan Das Kakkar

Acknowledgements

The title of the book "Humour in the lives of Great Men" reveals itself that the author of the book Dr. Jagdish Chandra Sharma – my beloved husband really lived humour. No storm could sink his boat. He could face big challenges with 1000 Watt Smile. This trait enabled him to work for eighteen hours a day and combine work with beauty as well as achieve excellence in every walk of life.

Though he was a victim of a serious disease yet he dedicated, devoted and completed the book with indomitable courage and splendid enthusiasm keeping in view the taste and demand of the readers around the globe. An ill-fated day came and the noble soul of my dear husband left all of us along with his dearest book which was yet to be published. I am deeply indebted to my well-wishers, colleagues, scholars and talented friends—such as Mrs. Asha Ahuja and Mr. M.L. Ahuja (The author of several books.) Mrs. Savita Khanna and Mr. Wazir Chand Khanna (Senior Lecturer in English Govt. College Faridabad.) Mrs. Shashi Datta and Mr. B.M. Datta (Retd Principal K.V.S.) Mrs. Raj Mahajan and Mr. R.C. Gupta (Director Corporate Office, Shivalik Agropoly Products Ltd., Mohali) for their valuable contribution for completing all formalities to get the book published. I am highly grateful for my dear and near one's.

I bless from the core of my heart my younger brother Dr. K.K. Bhutani (H.O.D. Computer Deptt. Allahabad. University) Sunita Bhutani (Sister-in-law), Mrs. Prabha Khosla (Younger Sister), Mr. Sunil Bhatia and Dr. Vijay Kakkar (Sons-in-law), Mrs. Sumita Bhatia and Dr. Sangeeta Kakkar (Daughters) Mr. Manu Chandra (Son), Mrs. Renu Chandra (daughter-in-law) Snigdha Bhatia, Shruti Kakkar, Saksham Kakkar, Shreya Bhatia, Smridha Chandra, Sneha

Chandra (Grand children). They all have fortified me emotionally by infusing strength to overcome the grief through their love, regard, respect, care and unending support. Their love for their father and grand father speaks volumes of values, they practise.

Last but not the least I am extremely thankful to Shri Ashok Kumar Mittal of Concept Publishing Company Pvt. Ltd. for bringing out the book with imposing get up as desired by my beloved husband who consistently remembered Ashokjee during his last days for the book to see the light of the day when darkness had prevailed around him.

In the end I would express my profound gratitude for one and all who had contributed their mite enabling me to place the book in their hands. May God bless them all with long, healthy, happy and, prosperous life.

Kailash Chandra
w/o Late Dr. Jagdish Chandra Sharma
C2B/59A Janakpuri.
New Delhi-110058

Contents

Acknowledgements vii
Introduction xiii

1. General **1**
- The Two Wolves 1
- Politics 1
- Fame 2
- Communism 3
- Bachelorhood 4
- Familiarity 5
- Mother-in-Law 6
- Music 7

2. Jawaharlal Nehru **8**
- Ramblings of Nehru on Different Topics 8
- Mathematics in Ancient India 8
- Religion 16
- Hindu Religion 17

3. Mahatma Gandhi **18**
- Silence 23
- Life 23
- Valour-Bravery 24
- Satyagrah 24
- Time 25
- Truth 25
- Woman 25
- Obedience 25

■ Non-Violence 26
■ Practice 26
■ Prayer 26
■ Religion 26

4. **Bernard Shaw and Churchill** **28**

5. **Generals and other Bigwigs** **32**
■ Jurisdiction 33
■ Justice 35
■ Tact 43

6. **Albert Einstein** **51**
■ Little Known Facts 54
■ The Theory of Relativity 56
■ Einstein Lover Uncovered 56
■ Einstein and XU 57
■ Life Comes from a Beautiful Mind 58

7. **Some Other Dignitaries** **62**
■ Alexander Dumas 62
■ Charles Darwin 63
■ Edgar Allan Poe 64
■ Writer of Alice in Wonderland 65
■ Catherine 66
■ Charlie Chaplin 66
■ Columbus 67
■ Thomas A. Edison 68
■ H.G. Wells 70
■ O. Henry 71
■ Josephine and Napoleon 72
■ Lenin 73
■ Abraham Lincoln 76

- Pt. Madan Mohan Malviya on Nizam of Hyderabad 79
- The Richest Man in the World Eats Soup with his Fingers 80
- Walt Disney 82
- Coleridge 82
- John Lamb 83
- Sir Robert Walpole 83
- P.B. Shelley 83
- Churchill 84
- Milton 84
- William Thackray 85
- A Miscellany 86

Introduction

The author of this book, Late Dr Jagdish Chandra Sharma, my father, was a practising homoeopathic physician. He took it as his hobby after he retired from his teaching career. He was blessed with sense of wit and humour. When he used to talk to his patients, a smile invariably radiated on his face. His sense of humour and jokes had the impact of removing most of the afflictions of his patients. With his sense of humour he was able to endear himself to the people around him. He used to spend most of his spare time in reading books, writing poetry and making notes. Even during his last days, while on bed, he continued to pour on books. The result is the compilation of several pieces, which, he felt, when published, should have therapeutic impact on the afflicted minds. These classified pieces of humour form the subject matter of this book. Though these excerpts reflect the sense of humour in the lives of some persons who rose to eminence at one time or the other in human history, yet some others are general in nature.

Humour and Laughter

What does humour mean and how it alleviates the sufferings of the audience? Papa, as I used to call my revered father, used to tell us that laughter is a physiological response to humour. It is a powerful form of exercise that gives us more of a cardiovascular workout than many 'regular' aerobic activities. He said that humour is the tendency of particular cognitive experiences to provoke laughter, provide amusement and alleviate most of our sufferings. In simple words, laughter is the physical response to humour. Laughter consists of two parts: a set of gestures and the production of a sound. When we laugh, the brain pressures us to conduct both these activities simultaneously. When we laugh heartily, changes occur in many parts of the body, even in the arm, leg and trunk muscles.

In this way, humour is the tendency of particular cognitive experiences to provoke laughter and provide amusement. People of all ages and cultures respond to humour. The majority of people are able to be amused, to laugh or smile at something funny, and thus they are considered to have a sense of humour. In ancient Sanskrit drama, Bharata Muni's *Natya Shastra* defined humour *(hasyam)* as one of the eight *nava rasyas,* or principal *rasas* (emotional responses) which can be inspired in the audience by *bhavas,* the imitations of emotions that the actors perform. Each *rasa* was associated with a specific *bhava* portrayed on stage. In the case of humour, it was associated with mirth *(hasya).* There is ample available literature to cause wit and humour in us. It is an art. Many plays are enacted in theatres which are intended to remove the stress caused in our everyday life. Many *hasya kavis* have written poetry which instantly sends peels of laughter among the audiences besides keeping them spellbound while they listen to them, thus inculcating in them the characteristic of attentiveness. Films with roles of comedians are largely preferred.

A sense of humour, Papa said, is the ability to experience humour, although the extent to which an individual finds something humorous depends on a host of variables. For instance, young children may possibly favour slapstisck, such as Punch and Judy puppet shows or cartoons, e.g. Tom and Jerry. Satire may rely more on understanding the target of the humour, and thus tends to appeal to more mature audiences. Nonsatirical humour can be specifically termed 'recreational drollery.'

Papa used to explain to us that humour occurs when the brain recognizes a pattern that surprises it, and that recognition of this sort is rewarded with the experience of the humorous response, an element of which is broadcast as laughter. An ability to recognize patterns instantly and unconsciously has proved a fundamental weapon in the cognitive arsenal of human beings. The humorous reward has encouraged the development of such faculties, leading to the unique perceptual and intellectual abilities of our species. Therefore, it has been used as a therapeutic effect, to some extent, for treating patients and as a device for criticism. It has been a powerful tool in bringing out social and religious reforms. The humourist takes the people to task for their failings. The humour of Eastern Europe, we are told, had been centered on defending the poor against the exploitation of the upper classes or other authorities. A number of reforms have used humour to convey their points effectively. Sant Kabir, for instance, ridiculed the external rituals as meaningless: smearing the body with ashes, taking a ritual bath thrice a day, keeping fasts and going on pilgrimage, flaunting rosaries, repeating God's name loudly and indulging in physical mortification. He said, if by wearing a holy thread a person could be called twice-born, why not call the iron-wheel in the well that always wears a rope?' At another place, he said, 'Why does the *kazi* shout so loudly, standing on the top of the minaret during his morning prayer? Has Allah gone deaf?' The speeches of Atal Bihari Vajpayee, former Prime Minister of India, in our own time, are also known for their punch and humour. With humour he has been able to strike his point instantly. Thus, reformers through the ages have been able to highlight the futility of some practices through their writings and sayings laced with humour.

Therapeutic Effects

Laughter activates the chemistry of the will to live. It increases our capacity to fight disease. Laughing relaxes the body and reduces problems associated with high blood pressure, strokes, arthritis, and ulcers, Papa once said. Some research suggests that laughter may also reduce the risk of heart disease. Historically, research has shown that distressing emotions (depression, anger, anxiety, and stress) are all related to heart disease. A study conducted at the University of Maryland Medical Center suggests that a good sense of humour and the ability to laugh at stressful situations helps mitigate the damaging physical effects of distressing emotions.

Laughter, as per the notes Papa has left behind, lowers the blood pressure. People, he felt, who laugh heartily on a regular basis, have lower blood pressure than any average person. When people have a good laugh, initially the blood pressure increases, but then it decreases to levels below normal. Breathing then becomes deeper which sends oxygen-enriched blood and nutrients throughout the body. Laughter decreases stress hormones and increases infection fighting antibodies. It increases our attentiveness, heart rate, and pulse. Laughter, along with an active sense of humour, may help protect us against a heart attack. It can be a great workout for our diaphragm, abdominal, respiratory, facial, leg, and back muscles. It massages abdominal organs, tones intestinal functioning, and strengthens the muscles that hold the abdominal organs in place.

Effects on Brain

Again, laughter stimulates both sides of the brain to enhance learning. It eases muscle tension and psychological stress, which keeps the brain alert and allows people to retain more information. A researcher, Derks, traced the pattern of brainwave activity in subjects responding to humorous material. Subjects were hooked up to an electroencephalograph (EEG) and their brain activity was measured the persons laughed. In each case, the brain produced a regular electrical pattern. Within four-tenths of a second of exposure to something potentially funny, an electrical wave moved through the cerebral cortex, the largest part of the brain. If the wave took a negative charge, laughter resulted. If it maintained a positive charge, no response was given, researchers said.

During the experiment, researchers observed that the left side of the cortext (the layer of cells that covers the entire surface of the forebrain) analyzed the words and structure of the joke; the brain's large frontal lobe, which is involved in social, emotional responses became very active. The right hemisphere of the cortext carried out the intellectual analysis required to get the joke. Brainwave activity then spread to the sensory processing area of the occipital lobe, the area on the back of the head that contains the cells that process visual signals. Stimulation of the motor sections evoked physical response to the joke.

Under certain conditions, our bodies perform some rhythmic,

vocalized, expiratory and involuntary actions, which are better known as laughter. Fifteen facial muscles contract and stimulation of the Zygomatic major muscle (the main lifting mechanism of our upper lip) occurs. Meanwhile, the respiratory system is upset by the epiglottis half-closing the larynx so that air intake occurs irregularly, making us gasp. In extreme circumstances, the tear ducts are activated so that while the mouth is opening and closing and the struggle for oxygen intake continues, the face becomes moist and often red (or purple). The noises that usually accompany this bizarre behaviour range from sedate giggles to boisterous guffaws.

Sharing Laughter and Movement

John Morreal believes that the first human laughter might have begun as a gesture of shared relief at the passing of danger. And since the relaxation that results from a bout of laughter inhibits the biological fight-or-flight response, laughter may indicate trust in one's companions. Many researchers believe that the purpose of laughter is related to making and strengthening human connections. In fact, laughter occurs when people are comfortable with one another, when they feel open and free. And the more laughter there is, the more bonding occurs with the group. Studies have also found that dominant individuals—the boss, the tribal chief or the family patriarch—use humour more than their subordinates.

Why the laughing movement is spreading so fast? Today, many people fear widespread international terrorism and our life has become quite stressful taking toll of many lives due to cardiac arrest. Laughter is a positive and powerful emotion that has all the ingredients required for individuals to change themselves and to change the world in a peaceful and positive way. It directly impacts one's electromagnetic field and creates a positive aura around us. When a group of individuals laugh together, they create a collective community aura. Electromagnetic waves from a group of people, who are laughing every day, form a protective envelope around that area to protect it from negative forces. Laughter is a universal language which has the potential to unite humanity without religion.

On March 1995, Dr Madan Kataria, a family physician from Mumbai, India, decided to write an article called "Laughter: The Best Medicine" for his monthly health magazine, *My Family Doctor.* His desk researched him to discover an overwhelming body of scientific literature that described in great length the proven benefits of laughter on the human mind and body. He was very impressed particularly by American journalist Norman Cousins' book, *Anatomy of an Illness,* and the research work undertaken by Dr Berk from Loma Linda University. He was profoundly inspired and being a man of action rather than an academic, he immediately decided to field-test the impact of laughter on himself.

Laughing Clubs

At 7 am the next morning, Dr Kataria went to his local public park and somehow managed to motivate four people to start a laughter club. This small group quickly grew to over 50 participants within a few days. In the beginning, everybody stood in a circle while one person would come to the center and crack a joke or tell a humorous anecdote. Everybody enjoyed the fun and felt nice for the rest of the day. After about two weeks, however, the stock of good jokes ran out and the 'bad', hurtful, sexist jokes came up. Two women were offended and complained. It became clear that an alternative to jokes had to be found if this laughter club was to survive.

Dr Kataria re-read the scientific research he had on laughter and found the answer he was looking for: the human mind doesn't know how to make a distinction between fake and genuine laughter. Either way, it produces happy chemistry. The concept of laughing for no reason was evolved. His wife, Madhuri Kataria, brought in her experience as a yoga teacher, and suggested gentle breathing and other yoga exercises to be included in the routine to deepen its impact.

In this way, Dr. Kataria was the first one to discover and make use of the fact that any one can laugh for 15-20 minutes without depending upon a sense of humour or comedy. We do not need to be happy, have a sense of humour or even have any reason to laugh.

Laughter Yoga bases itself on the philosophy of acting happiness. We simulate to stimulate. At times, fake laughter becomes genuine and flows like a fountain. Laughter Yoga crosses all barriers: age, gender, language, culture, physical abilities, race, religion, political beliefs, etc. Laughter is part of the universal human vocabulary. All members of the human species understand it.

The resulting Laughter Yoga technique is a blend of yogic deep breathing, stretching, simulated laughter exercises and cultivated child-like playfulness. Looking at the impact of laughing on the health of the people, Swami Ramdev in India has started a movement. Though his movement is intended to be an exposition of Patanjali's system of yoga, which laid down its principles long back, laughing is one of the exercises included in the yoga curriculum, when Swami Ramdev makes people laugh for a few minutes. His programmes on T.V. and in various States of India are being widely appreciated. They have benefited many people in the country.

Outside India also, laughter has assumed sufficient significance to the extent of organizing World Laughter Day on the first Sunday of May, every year. Hundreds of people, rather thousands, gather worldwide on that day to laugh together. Such an enthusiastic participation is proof that Laughter Club movement, started with just five persons in 1995, has grown into a worldwide movement with more than 5,000 clubs in countries like India, USA, Canada, Australia, U.K, France, Germany, Italy, Belgium, Switzerland, Sweden, Norway, Denmark, Hungary, Ireland, the Netherlands, Finland, Singapore, Indonesia, Malaysia, Vietnam, Taiwan, Hong Kong and Dubai. Laughter yoga clubs have been covered by prestigious television channels like BBC, CNN, ABC (USA), NHK (Japan), Channel 7&9 (Australia), and newspapers, magazines like *National Geographic, New York Times, London Times, The Wall Street Journal* and many others.

Of course, too much of everything is not good. We have not to laugh too much and put our body into distress. A typical laughter yoga session lasts about 20 to 30 minutes. Anything beyond 30 minutes is in the red zone and may adversely affect some people, especially the seniors. Let us use our common sense; we have not to put unnecessary strain on our body to cause pain. It is also not good to laugh at people for something for which the person laughed at cannot help. Our laughing should not mean hurting the sentiments of somebody. It is not good to laugh at somebody when he/she is in distress.

The following pages of this book contain excerpts collected by Papa from the writings and sayings of some people who, in their lives have attained eminence because of their distinguished contribution in one field or the other. They should serve as tools of information while invoking a sense of humour. The information cited above is based on Papa's diary who felt that humour acts as therapeutic medicine. I hope that this book should be a valuable repository of information and the readers will feel enlightened and enjoy its contents. For me it will be a greatest tribute to my father if its contents can benefit even some of the people.

St. Louis, USA
August 15, 2009

Manu Chandra

1

General

The Two Wolves

An elderly Cherokee Native, American was telling something to his grandchildren about life. He told them, "A fight is going on inside me...it is a terrible fight, and it is between two wolves. One wolf represents fear, anger, envy, sorrow, regret, greed, arrogance, self-pity, guilt, resentment, inferiority, lies, pride and superiority. The other wolf stands for joy, peace, love, hope, sharing, serenity, humility, kindness, benevolence, friendship, empathy, generosity, truth, compassion and faith. This same fight is going on inside you and every other person too."

They thought about it for a minute and then one child asked his grandfather, "Which wolf will win?" The old Cherokee simply replied, "The one I feed."

—*Times of India*, 11, July, 2006

Politics

A Texas oilman offered to throw the biggest goldarmed victory party for Thomas E. Dewey, this country or any other country ever saw. "It'll be a two-hundred-and-fifty-thousand-dollar complimentary banquet in honour of Dewey's election to the office of President of the United States," he said.

"Fine," said a friend. "But supposing he doesn't/don't win the election."

The Texan replied, "Then we'll have the complimentary banquet in honour of his defeat."

• Governor Robert Bradford of Massachusetts set down these attributes for a successful politician:

"To live long in politics, you must possess the hide of a rhinoceros, the memory of an elephant, the persistence of a beaver, the native friendliness of a mongrel pup. You need the heart of a lion and the stomach of an ostrich. And it helps to have the humour and ubiquity of the crow. But all of these combined are not enough, unless when it comes to matters of principle, you also have the stubbornness of an army mule."

• George E. Allen, once President Eisenhower's golf and bridge buddy, said that President Roosevelt liked best this joke on himself. A dyed-in-the-wool New Deal-hater in Westchester commuted to *New York daily* and damned Roosevelt every inch of the way. Reaching Grand Central, he always rushed to the newsstand, bought a *Times*, glanced over the front page and handed it back to the news dealer. Finally, the dealer asked him why he never looked at the inside of the paper.

"I'm only interested in finding a certain obituary", the enemy said.

"But the obituaries are on page 24," the dealer suggested.

"The so and so I'm looking for," said the man of firm habit, "will be on page one."

—J.M. Braude, *Wit and Humour*

Fame

• An old man living in an apartment with his grandson heard that Jascha Heifetz had moved next door. He was so overcome with emotion at the news that he ran into Heifetz's apartment and said, "Oh, Mr. Heifetz, to think that such a great man as yourself is living next door to me. I can't believe it! My grandson will be overjoyed—he worships you."

Heifetz, wanting to be a good neighbour, offered to play his violin for the grandson, whereupon the old man said, "Oh—you play the fiddle, too?"

- "What's your name?" asked the store manager of the young boy who was applying for a job.

"Ford," replied the lad.

"And your first name?"

"Henry."

"Henry Ford, eh?" queried the manager with a smile. "That's pretty well known name."

The boy looked pleased. "Yes, sir, it should be," he replied proudly. "I've been delivering groceries around town for two years now."

Communism

- A German and a Russian were fishing on opposite side of the river. The German caught fish after fish, while the Russian didn't even get a bite.

Finally, the Russian yelled across, "Why is it you catch fish and I get none?"

The German thought a minute and then replied, "I guess on your side they are afraid to open their mouths."

- Three cellmates in a Soviet hoosegow compared notes.

"I was jailed for coming late to work," mourned the first.

"Me? I came too early," recounted the second. "They said this proved I was a Capitalist spy."

"And I'm here," complained the third, "because I arrived exactly on time. They accused me of owning an American watch."

• A French poodle met a Russian wolfhound on the Champs Elysees in Paris. "How are things in Russia?" asked the French poodle.

"Fabulous," the Russian wolfhound replied. "I sleep in a solid gold dog house on a sable carpet, and all day long they feed me caviar."

"Well," asked the French poodle, "if things are so good in Russia, why do you come to Paris?" The Russian wolfhound leaned forward. "Well," he whispered confidentially, "sometimes I like to bark."

• A Moscow father was complimenting another on his three sons.

"You must be mighty proud of them," he said. "One a people's doctor, one a people's lawyer, and one a people's artist."

"Yes, they're fine boys", said the father, "but the son I'm really proud of is in America."

"Oh, he's an American?"

—J.M. Braude, "*Wit and Humour*"

Bachelorhood

• The only thing worse than being a bachelor is being a bachelor's son.

• *Prospective employee*: "Just why do you want a married man to work for you rather than a bachelor?"

Boss: "The married men don't get so upset if I yell at them."

• "I was sorry to hear that your brother passed on," one old classmate consoled another at a reunion. "Had he finished his education?"

"No," said the other. "He died as bachelor."

• The bachelor's attractive new housekeeper tiptoed into the study and asked apologetically, "Sir, shall I clean your stove and sweep your porch now?"

"Margie," said the bachelor, "in this house we are all for one and one for all. You do not say 'your stove' or 'your porch' or 'your chair'. Instead, you say 'our stove', 'our porch' or 'your chair.'"

That evening Margie served a splendid dinner to the bachelor and his boss and the boss's daughter, whom the bachelor was anxious to impress.

Margie was late in serving the last course and she rushed into the dining room and excitedly announced: "I'm sorry I was late, sir, but I was upstairs chasing a mouse from under 'our bed.'

—J.M. Braude, "*Wit and Humour*"

Familiarity

● A small boy went with his family for a visit of several days in New York City and of all the sights they saw his big favourite was the majestic statue of General Sherman on horseback at Fifth Avenue and 59th Street.

He asked to be taken back to the statue several times and every time he went, he asked countless questions about the great Northern general. On the trip back to his home he was still cross-examining his father on the details of Sherman's deeds in the Civil War.

"But, Daddy, there's one thing I don't understand," he said finally. "Who is that man who was sitting on General Sherman?"

● An editor, weary of the abuse following his editorials, ran the Ten Commandments in his editorial column.

A few days later came a letter: "Cancel my subscription. You're getting too personal."

• The doctor had been called to look over Grandma, who had been complaining of aches and pains. He gave her a thorough going-over.

After he left, Grandma seemed to perk up a bit. "What did you say was the name of that new minister?" she asked.

"That wasn't the minister—that was the doctor", she was told.

"Hmmm, I thought he was a bit familiar for a minister," Grandma replied.

Mother-in-Law

• The modern girl usually gets along fine with her mother-in-law because she can't afford another baby sitter.

• Sometimes you can't tell if a man is trying so hard to be a success is to please his wife or to spite his mother-in-law.

• A newly-married man found his wife in tears when he arrived home from the office.

"You know that cake I made from mother's recipe?" she sobbed. "Well, I put it out to cool and the cat ate half of it."

"Never mind, darling," he comforted. "I know someone who will give us a kitten."

• A big game hunter went to Africa with his wife and his mother-in-law. They hired a guide who took them on a safari into the wilds of the jungle. One night, about a week after they were out, the husband and his wife awoke and discovered that mama was missing. After searching an hour for her, they were shocked to find her cowering in a clearing with a huge lion standing over her.

"Oh, what are we going to do?" the horrified wife asked.

"Nothing," answered the husband. "The lion got himself into that fix—now let him get out of it."

• The young wife was in tears when she opened the door for her husband. "I've been insulted," she sobbed. "Your mother insulted me."

"My mother!" he exclaimed. "But she is a hundred miles away."

"I know, but a letter came for you this morning and I opened it."

He looked stern. "I see, but where does the insult come in?"

"In the postscript," she answered. "It said: 'Dear Alice, don't forget to give this letter to George'."

Music

• The village band finished a vigorous and not overharmonious selection. As the perspiring musicians sank to their seats after acknowledging the applause, the trombonist asked, "What's the next number?"

The leader replied, "The Washington Post March."

"Oh, no," gasped the trombonist. "I just got through playing that!"

• At a large party a Hollywood hostess decided to sing. In an off-pitch voice she rendered **Carry Me Back to Old Virginee.** She really belted the song, and as she sang, she noticed a distinguished, white-haired guest bow his head and weep quietly. When she finished the hostess approached the old man and said, "Pardon me, sir, but are you a Virginian?"

"No, ma'am," said the elderly guest, wiping away a tear. "I'm a musician."

2

Jawaharlal Nehru

Ramblings of Nehru on Different Topics

- Little baby squirrels would sometimes fall down from the trees. The mother would come after them, roll them up into a little ball, and carry them off to safety. Occasionally the baby got lost. One of my companions picked up three of these lost baby squirrels and looked after them. They were so tiny that it was a problem how to feed them. The problem was, however, solved rather ingeniously. A fountain-pen filler, with a little cotton wool attached to it, made an efficient feeding bottle.

—Jawaharlal Nehru, *An Autobiography*, p. 356, Lucknow Gaol (Jail)

Mathematics in Ancient India

- Highly intellectual and given to abstract thinking as they were, one would expect the ancient Indians to excel in mathematics. Europe got its early arithmetic and algebra from the Arabs—hence the 'Arabic numerals'—but the Arabs themselves had previously taken them from India. The astonishing progress that the Indians had made in mathematics is now well known and it is recognized that the foundations of modern arithmetic and algebra were laid long ago in India. The clumsy method of using a counting frame and the use of Roman and such like numerals had long retarded progress when the ten Indian numerals, including the zero sign, liberated the human mind from these restrictions and threw a flood of light on the behaviour of numbers.

—Jawaharlal Nehru, *the Discovery of India*

• Even if God did not exist, it would be necessary to invent him, so Voltaire said—'si Dieu n'existait pas, il faudrait l'inventer.' Perhaps that is true, and indeed the mind of man has always been trying of fashion some such mental image or conception which grew with the mind's growth. But there is something also in the reverse proposition: even if God exists, it may be desirable not to look up to Him or to rely upon Him. Too much dependence on supernatural factors may lead, and has often led, to a loss of self-reliance in man and to a blunting of his capacity and creative ability. And yet some faith seems necessary in things of the spirit which are beyond the scope of our physical world, some reliance on moral, spiritual, and idealistic conceptions, or else we have no anchorage, no objectives or purpose in life.

—Jawaharlal Nehru, *The Discovery of India,* p. 513

• In Naini there were thousands of parrots, and large numbers of them lived in the crevices of my barrack walls. Their courtship and love-making was always a fascinating sight, and sometimes there were fierce quarrels between two male parrots over a lady parrot, who sat calmly by waiting for the result of the encounter and ready to grant her favours to the winner.

—Jawaharlal Nehru, *An Autobiography*, p. 388, Naini Jail

• Picture books also entertain, especially of mountains and glaciers and deserts, for in prison one hungers for wide spaces and seas and mountains. I had some beautiful picture books of Mont Blanc, the Alps, and the Himalayas, and I turned to them often and gazed at the glaciers when the temperature of my cell or barrack was 115°F or even more. An atlas was an exciting affair. It brought all manner of past memories and dreams of places we had visited and places we had wanted to go to.

—Jawaharlal Nehru, *An Autobiography*, p. 352

• There was little sympathy with the British in spite of loud professions of loyalty. Moderate and Extremist alike learnt with satisfaction German victories. There was no love for Germany, of course, only the desire to see our own rulers humbled. It was the weak and helpless man's idea of vicarious revenge. I suppose most of us viewed the struggle with mixed feelings. Of all the nations involved my sympathies were probably most with France. The ceaseless and unabashed propaganda on behalf of the Allies had some effect, although we tried to discount it greatly.

—Jawaharlal Nehru, *An Autobiography,* p. 31

• Jim Phelan in his 'Jail Journey' tells us of the effect of jail on human character, and everyone who has spent a long time in prison knows how true his statement is: 'The jail...acts as a magnifying glass on human character. Every tiny weakness is brought out, emphasized, weakened, until presently there is no more of the convict with the weakness but only a weakness wearing convict clothes.' Some such effect is produced on national character by foreign rule. That is not the only effect, for noble qualities also develop and strength is gradually built up through resistance.

—Jawaharlal Nehru, *The Discovery of India,* p. 527

• Different countries have adopted different animals as symbols of their ambition or character—the eagle of the United States of America and of Germany, the lion and bulldog of England, the fighting-cock of France, the bear of old Russia. How far do these patron animals mould national character? Most of them are aggressive, fighting animals, beasts of prey. It is not surprising that the people who grow up with these examples before them should mould themselves consciously after them and strike up aggressive attitudes, and roar, and prey on others. Nor is it surprising that the Hindu should be mild and non-violent, for his patron animal is the cow.

—Jawaharlal Nehru, *An Autobiography*, p. 359

• There was a large colony of monkeys in Bareilly Gaol and their antics were always worth watching. One incident impressed me. A baby monkey managed to come down into our barrack enclosure and he could not mount up the wall again. The warder and some convict overseers and other prisoners caught hold of him and tied a bit of string round his neck. The parents (presumably) of the little one saw all this from the top of the high wall, and their anger grew. Suddenly one of them, a huge monkey, jumped down and charged almost right into the crowd which surrounded the baby monkey. It was an extraordinary brave thing to do, for the warden and C.O.'s had sticks and *lathis* and they were brandishing them about, and there was quite a crowd of them. Reckless courage triumphed, and the crowd of humans fled, terrified, leaving their sticks behind them! The little monkey was rescued.

—Jawaharlal Nehru, *An Autobiography*, p. 356

• Nehru had ingratiated himself so much with his people that at the time of his death a good number of persons died of shock; many fainted, the innumerable people felt as if they had become orphans. The voluntary 'hartal' was observed for two days. At Gandhi's death there was only a single day's 'hartal'. A few persons had fainted but deaths out of shock were not many. We may account for this phenomenon by declaring that while Gandhi was worshipped by the people, Nehru was loved by them.

• On reaching New York during a visit, he felt the urge to meet Dr. Einstein who was then residing at the University of Princeton. He cancelled a few engagements to see him. He also went to felicitate John Dewey, the Philosopher, on his birthday. He also sought to meet Robert Frost, the Poet.

He was happy in the company of poets, novelists, scientists, philosophers, actors, painters and the like; and often complained that some politicians and plutocrats gave him pain in the neck!

- Jawaharlal, as everyone knows, was children's darling. The children always struck a highly responsive chord in Nehru's heart. "The children of a nation," he said, "are a trust of the nation. What the future, will be, depends on how we discharge this trust". Whenever he felt worried or troubled by cares of the State, he sought and found peace and solace amidst them. In fact, child in Nehru was always strong. His birthday (November 14) has been turned into Children's Day according to his declared wish. On this day he played, sang and danced with children. Admitting his delight on such occasions, he once wrote: 'I like being with children and talking with them and even more, playing with them. For a moment, I forget that I am terribly old and that it is a very long time ago since I was a child.'

Children, but because these children who will grow up, will be the future citizens of India. It pained me to see that some of these children are not properly looked after and attended to. I think all of us have a certain responsibility to see that children in the country are properly looked after.

- Years ago, addressing a meeting at Ewing Christian College, Allahabad, Mr. Lal Bahadur Shastri, the then Prime Minster, related a story about Nehru's considerate nature. After an election meeting in 1937 he said, Nehru was returning to Allahabad with a couple of comrades. He himself was driving the car. It was a cold winter night and there was fog all-round. It was difficult to drive, but he decided to take every comrade home. As he was driving along a cow crossed the way and despite his best efforts the car hit the animal, breaking one of its horns. It was dark, and perhaps none noticed the incident, but Nehru stopped the car to meet the owner of the cow. After a few minutes some people passed that way and when they saw Nehru worrying about this affair, they requested him to get along and not to bother. But he did not leave before he made them promise to send the owner of the cow to Anand Bhawan next morning. When the man came and met Nehru, he got a substantial sum for the treatment of his injured cow.

- Nehru loved hard work. He was always immensely busy in his work. Even when he was not the Prime Minister, he used to do a lot of work and very often, despite his good health, he felt very tired. On July 27, 1942, he called Shri P.D. Tandon, a journalist, to his study room in the afternoon to dictate something for the press. He started dictating, but he felt asleep in the midst of it. Mr. Tandon quietly sat watching his face. Nehru relaxed on a comfortable arm-chair and snatched a few minutes of rest! When he woke up, he asked for how long he had slept and had he (Tandon) to wait for long? Mr. Tandon told Panditji that he had dozed only for a few minutes. He wished him to rest a little longer as he seemed to be very tired. Mr. Nehru refused to go into slumber again and said that he did not think so and that he was quite fresh. Thereafter he continued the work.

- He disliked Delhi but had to stay there. Speaking of Delhi he once observed, "I do not know what effect a fairly lengthy residence in Delhi might have upon us, because it has been my experience that it has very numbing effect on individuals, and results in a weakening of their intellectual and certainly their physical faculties. Maybe, we might be affected that way, but I hope not. New Delhi, as it has been constituted thus far, is something unique in India and something apart from India. It does not represent India although it contains many eminent Indians. How far it is possible to change this atmosphere of New Delhi and bring it more into live touch with the real

Indian atmosphere, I do not know, and it is up to all of us to try to do so."

- Nehru got furious and unhappy when stories of gross administrative incompetence were brought to his notice. In October 1953 a few pensioners visited Anand Bhawan to complain to Nehru that they had not received their pensions for the last four or five years. The shivering, thin, old man attracted a lot of sympathy at Anand Bhawan that day and almost everybody advised them to place their case before the Prime Minister. Even the officials present there felt somewhat ashamed.

The Prime Minister came out to meet the visitors and politely enquired of them what was the matter. One of the pensioners almost broke down and with a trembling voice said, "Sir, we have not got our pensions for the last four years. We are dying of hunger." Nehru was shocked and exclaimed "What? You haven't got your pensions for the last four years." The pensioners bowed respectfully and replied, "Sir, whatever we are saying is correct. You can ask the District Magistrate". Instantly the Magistrate was called and Nehru on seeing him asked indignantly, "Do you hear what they say? This is shocking; this is incredible! What have you to say about it?"

The District Magistrate tried to explain things but Nehru interrupted, "Explanations will not do. See to it that they get their pensions without any further delay."

- He did not believe in smiles to order. During one of his visits to the United States, he was received by President Truman at the airport. After the ceremonies of Guard of Honour and Speech-making were over, Truman escorted him to the car where cameramen were awaiting the couple. One cameraman shouted "Mr. Prime Minister, give us a good broad smile. Sure you are happy with us!"

Truman opened up into a very broad smile and whispered to Nehru to do the same. Nehru sulked, frowned and became increasingly serious. "They can't have smiles to order and I, for one, will not be ordered when and how to smile." And then suddenly he burst into the most hilarious laughter.

- One day Mr. P.D. Tandon, the Journalist, told the Prime Minister in New York that there was a lot of repetition in most of his major speeches and the pressmen were feeling bored. At once retorted the Prime Minister, "I do not tire of seeing all of you everyday at all the meetings. Do I?"

- Nehru had great weakness for the Himalayas. In an all-important room in Teen Murti House, the pride of place is given to a painting of the mighty Himalayan peaks which Nehru adored throughout his life. "I know of no other place in the world has much tremendous power locked up in it as the Himalayas," he would often say.

- Mr. Jai Singh, Member of Parliament, once organized a cricket-match to help the flood victims in Andhra Pradesh and Punjab. Mr. Nehru led one team while Dr. Radhakrishnan led the other. In this match, Panditji took a very difficult catch at point, the batsman being Keshav Dev Malaviya. Later, when he was batting, he had as his partner the communist leader, A.K. Gopalan and made three runs not out. This was a living example of his doctrine, 'Peaceful Co-existence'. Mr. Vizzy, the commentator, requested Nehru to come to the commentator's box and say a few words over the 'mike'. After a short speech, he began a commentary on the proceedings. It came as a surprise to everyone to discover that he was not only a sportsman, but also a sports' commentator.

- One Sunday in January 1951, the clerk at the Imperial Hotel, New Delhi, handed over a message to Norman Cousin from the Prime Minister. Mr. Norman, along with some invitees, reached the P.M.'s house at about 3 P.M. Mr. Nehru was at the door, welcoming his guests. He seemed to be in excellent spirits. All were ushered into a large enclosed verandah.

Then Mr. Nehru came into the room, his young grandson riding on his shoulders, kicking grandpa's ribs and demanding more speed. "The gallop comes later," Mr. Nehru said, hoisting the boy over his head and placing him on the floor. He told the youngster, "He had a surprise for everyone." A magic show had been arranged!

The Finance Minister was hesitant to be part of an item of the show. The Magician with his arrow, blind folded, was to cause the flower-wreath to fall around the Finance Minister's distinguished shoulders. Mr. Nehru spoke up, "They tell me that good Finance Ministers are hard to find these days. I don't know whether we ought to allow him to go through with this." When the magician assumed his shooting position and raised the bow and arrow, Mr. Nehru cried, "No, no, you are aiming at the wrong man. You are aiming at the Justice. We cannot afford to lose him. The man you want is about sixty degrees to the left. Suddenly, the magician let fly. The arrow pierced the string and the garland fell neatly over the shoulders of the Finance Minister."

Dr. Radhakrishnan, who was also present at the magic show, remarked inside the car on his way back home: "There is something eternally young, even boyish about the Prime Minister. People tend to think of him as a man lost in brooding not even knowing how to laugh. Not so, he loves to laugh, as we have seen. It is very good for the nation that he can laugh. It helps to freshen his spirits. The important thing about Nehru is that he continues to think young. A man like him can never grow old. He will never look old, no matter how old he is but he must take better care of himself. He works too hard."

Religion

No organized religion today will express itself in this out-spoken manner, but essentially its attitude to property and the existing social order will be the same.

Words are well known to be, by themselves, very imperfect means of communication, and are often understood in a variety of ways. No word perhaps in any language is more likely to be interpreted in different ways by different people as the word 'religion' (or the corresponding words in other languages). Probably no two persons will, have same complex of ideas and images, arise on hearing or reading this word. Among these ideas and images may be those of rites and ceremonial, of sacred books, of a community of people, of certain dogmas, of morals, reverence, love, fear, hatred, charity, sacrifice, asceticism, fasting, feasting, prayer, ancient history, marriage, death, the next world, of riots and the breaking of heads, and so on.

—Jawaharlal Nehru, *An Autobiography*, p. 378

Hindu Religion

The Hindu religion especially went up in my estimate; not the ritual or ceremonial part, but its great books, the "Upanishads" and the "Bhagavad-Gita". I don't understand them, of course, but they seemed very wonderful. I dreamt of astral bodies and imagined myself flying vast distances. This dream of flying high up in the air (without any appliance) has indeed been a frequent one throughout my life; and sometimes it has been vivid and realistic and the countryside seemed to be under me in a vast panorama. I do not know how the modern interpreters, Freud and others, would interpret this dream.

—Jawaharlal Nehru, *An Autobiography*, p.15

3

Mahatma Gandhi

Reckoned in terms of money, Gandhi was a poor man. If he sold all his earthly possessions, they probably would not bring seventy-five cents; yet he was more powerful than any millionaire on earth.

Physically, he was weak; and he refused to use force or violence; yet his teachings and his spiritual influence were more potent and powerful than a hundred battleships of England.

One person out of every six on earth lives in India. And for centuries, these people of India have been asleep; now this little, frail man, who weighed less than a hundred pounds, was arousing India to a sense of its own gigantic power! He was instituting reforms that might have far-reaching effects on the history of the world.

There were many curious things about Gandhi. For example, he had a set of false teeth, which he carried in a fold of his loin cloth. He put them in his mouth only when he wanted to eat. After his meal, he took them out, washed them and put them back in his loin cloth again.

He spoke English with an Irish accent.

• Gandhi had been greatly influenced by the teachings of an American by the name of David Thoreau. Thoreau had graduated from Harvard University ninety years ago, and then spent twenty-eight dollars building a cabin for himself on the lonely shores of Walden Pond, in Massachusetts. He lived there like a hermit, and refused to pay taxes; so he was thrown into jail. He then wrote a book on Civil Disobedience, saying that no one ought to pay taxes. People didn't pay the slightest attention to his book then; but, seventy-five years later, Gandhi read that book, away out in India, and decided to use Thoreau's tactics.

- Once some girls of the Ashram were found infested with lice. Gandhiji took the scissors and cut their hair off. When Kasturaba came to know of it, she became furious and chided Gandhiji for that foolishness. Gandhi was so much astounded that he began to tremble.

The teacher in Gandhiji came to the fore and he started classes to educate Kasturba and other girls in the Ashram. The girls had enough capacity for cramming things whereas Kasturba, being an old lady, had the weakness of forgetting her lessons. One day Gandhiji gave a test to his small class. The girls including his granddaughter got through the examination while Kasturba failed miserably. Being disappointed, he abandoned his futile attempt at educating his wife.

- One night Manu Gandhi (Gandhi's granddaughter) woke up at midnight and found the light on in the room of Gandhiji. She first went to his room to satisfy her curiosity. To her surprise, she found Gandhiji busy in search for something. To help her grandfather, she stepped in and enquired as to what the matter was. She was simply amazed at the answer as a stump of a pencil was reported to have been lost. She was unable to understand the importance of searching for a small piece of a lead pencil. She told him that she had an unused pencil which she would offer to him, but he refused to accept. He wanted the same old small piece which had served him well.

Manu Gandhi, one day lost a piece of stone used as paper-weight by Gandhiji, who on being aware of the loss sent her out to find it out. He could not rest till it was recovered.

- He never mitigated the importance of money in life. Like other great men, he did not condemn wealth. Rather he preached earning of wealth honestly and using it economically. Unlike other great men, he never felt shy of charging rupees five for one autograph.
- One of the inmates of the Ashram, who hailed from the South, fell ill. Gandhiji went to inquire about his health and as a matter of courtesy asked him what he wanted. The South Indian patient expressed his wish for a cup of coffee. Gandhiji went to the kitchen, prepared the coffee himself and brought it to him with the apology that perhaps he had not prepared the beverage well. The patient was simply astonished as he knew that coffee and tea were a taboo in Ashram.
- Gandhiji went to see Tagore at 'Shanti Niketan' who had decorated the room well in honour of the visiting dignitary. Being pleased with the decoration, Gandhiji remarked that the room appeared to have been adorned excellently for the wedding couple. He further remarked that the bride had come but where the bridegroom was!
- Gandhiji once asked Manu Gandhi to shave him off. She performed the act nicely. At that moment, Shri Rajagopalachari happened to come and was amused at the funny scene. Gandhi praised the barber's skill shown by Manu, where on Rajaji advised her to open a shaving saloon displaying a signboard with the words: "Certified by Mahatma Gandhi".

All this amply shows how simple at heart was the shrewd politician. He was innocent like a villager and meticulous like a householder and humorous like a believer in the worth of this life which is meant for being lived with gusto.

- Gandhi when quite young was tempted once to eat meat but, not strangely enough, he ate up his sleep. That night he could not sleep as he felt as though the goat was bleating in his belly. Thereafter he took a vow not to touch meat in future.

• Gandhi, the dark-complexioned was so poorly clad as to look like a coolie. One fashionable gentleman, after alighting from the railway train, mistook Gandhiji for a porter, called him and gave him his luggage to be carried outside the station. Mahatma, the coolie, did the desired service unhesitatingly and disappeared without waiting for remuneration. Next day, the same gentleman realized his mistake when he saw Gandhi delivering lecture in a meeting.

—Dale Carnegie, *Little Known Facts About Well-known People*

• Gandhiji once told an interviewer that if he had not had the gift of humour he might have committed suicide, or something to this effect. I would not presume to go so far, but life certainly would have been almost intolerable for me but for the humour and light touches that some people gave to it.

—Jawaharlal Nehru, *An Autobiography*, p. 207

• People who do not know Gandhiji personally and have only read his writings are apt to think that he is a priestly type, extremely puritanical, long-faced, Calvinistic, and a kill-joy, something like the "priests in black gowns walking their rounds." But his writings do him an injustice; he is far greater than what he writes, and it is not quite fair to quote what he has written and criticize it. He is the very opposite of the Calvinistic priestly type. His smile is delightful, his laughter infectious, and he radiates light-heartedness. There is something childlike about him which is full of charm. When he enters a room he brings a breath of fresh air with him which lightens the atmosphere.

—Jawaharlal Nehru, *An Autobiography*, p. 515

• Gandhi speaking on Non-violence, "I do believe that when there is only a choice between cowardice and violence, I would advise violence… I would rather have India resort to arms in order to defend her honour than that she should in a cowardly manner become or remain a helpless victim to her own dishonour. But I believe that non-violence is infinitely superior to violence, forgiveness is more manly than punishment.

"Forgiveness adorns a soldier. But abstinence is forgiveness only when there is power to punish; it is meaningless when it pretends to proceed from a helpless creature. A mouse hardly forgives a cat when it allows itself to be torn to pieces by her... But I do not believe India to be helpless, I do not believe myself to be a helpless creature...

"Let me not be misunderstood. Strength does not come from physical capacity. It comes from an indomitable will...

—Jawaharlal Nehru, *An Autobiography*, p. 83

- "Non-violence in its dynamic condition means conscious suffering. It does not mean meek submission to the will of the evil-doer, but it means the putting of one's whole soul against the will of the tyrant. Working under this law of our being, it is possible for a single individual to defy the whole might of an unjust empire to save his honour, his religion, his soul and lay the foundation for that empire's fall.

—Jawaharlal Nehru, *An Autobiography*, p. 84

- As for Gandhiji himself, he was a very difficult person to understand, sometimes his language was almost incomprehensible to an average modern. But we felt that we knew him quite well enough to realize that he was a great and unique man and a glorious leader, and having put our faith in him we gave him an almost blank cheque, for the time being at least. Often we discussed his fads and peculiarities among ourselves and said, half-humorously, that when Swaraj came these fads must not be encouraged.

—Jawaharlal Nehru, *An Autobiography*, pp. 72-73

- It is based on pure monism, the only ultimate reality in the metaphysical sense being the *Atman*, the Absolute Soul. That is the subject, all else is objective. How that Absolute Soul pervades everything, how the one appears as the many, and yet retains its wholeness, for the Absolute is indivisible and cannot be divided, all this cannot be accounted for by the processes of logical reasoning, for our minds are limited by the finite world. The Upanishad had described this *Atman*, if this can be called a description thus: 'Whole is that, whole (too) is this; from whole, whole cometh; take whole from whole, (yet) whole remains.'

—Jawaharlal Nehru, *The Discovery of India*

Silence

I must say that beyond occasionally exposing me to laughter, my constitutional shyness has been no disadvantage whatever. In fact, I can say that, on the contrary, it has been all to my advantage. My hesitancy in speech, which was once an annoyance, is now a pleasure. Its greatest benefit has been that it has taught me the economy of words. I have naturally formed the habit of restraining my thoughts. And I can now give myself the certificate that a thoughtless word hardly ever escapes my tongue or pen. I do not recollect ever having had to regret anything in my speech or writing. I have thus been spared many a mishap and waste of time.

—N.B. Sen, *Wit and Wisdom of Mahatma Gandhi,* p. 262

Life

Gandhi on life.

Life is but an endless series of experiments.
Life without love is death.
There only is life where is love.
Life is perpetual triumph over the grave.

Life is one indivisible whole.

Life for me would be a burden, if I were to make it a point of controverting every false report about me or distortion of my writing.

—N.B. Sen, *Wit and Wisdom of Mahatma Gandhi*, pp. 170-71

- Silence helps one to suppress one's anger as perhaps nothing else does. How is one to give vent to one's wrath if one is silent? Not by eyes. Surely not by physical violence, when one is pledged to non-violence. Not by writing, for the wrath would disappear in the very process of writing.

—N.B. Sen, *Wit and Wisdom of Mahatma Gandhi*, p. 264

Valour-Bravery

He who perishes, sword in hand, is no doubt brave; but who faces death without raising his little finger and without flinching is braver. The brave meet death with a smile on their lips, but they are circumspect all the same.

—N.B. Sen, *Wit and Wisdom of Mahatma Gandhi*, p. 300

To everything prevented all clear thinking. Even some of Gandhiji's phrases sometimes jarred upon me—thus his frequent reference to *Rama Raj* as a golden age which was to return. But I was powerless to intervene, and I consoled myself with the thought that Gandhiji used the words because they were well known and understood by the masses. He had an amazing knack of reaching the heart of the people.

—Jawaharlal Nehru, *An Autobiography*, pp. 72-73

Satyagrah

Satyagrah is gentle, it never wounds. *Satyagrah* is a relentless search for truth and determination to reach truth. It is an unmistakable mute prayer of an agonized soul.

—*Wit and Wisdom of Mahatma Gandhi,* p. 253

Time

Time is a merciless enemy, as it is also a merciless friend and healer.

—*Wit and Wisdom of Mahatma Gandhi,* p. 291.

Truth

Truth is like a vast tree, which yields more and more fruit, the more you nurture it. The deeper the search in the mine of truth, the richer the discovery of the gems buried there in the shape of of stones, for an ever greater variety of service.

—*Wit and Wisdom of Mahatma Gandhi,* p. 292.

Woman

Woman is described as man's better half. As long as she has not the same rights in law as man, as long as the birth of a girl does not receive the same welcome as that of a boy, so long we should know that India is suffering from partial paralyses. Suppression of woman is a denial of *Ahimsa.*

—*Wit and Wisdom of Mahatma Gandhi,* p. 318

Obedience

Compulsory obedience to a master is a state of slavery, willing obedience to one's father is the glory of sonship.

—*Wit and Wisdom of Mahatma Gandhi,* p. 206

Non-Violence

Ahimsa in education shines clear and far, and can no more be hidden by any means.

—*Wit and Wisdom of Mahatma Gandhi,* p. 198

Ahimsa and *Satya* are my two lungs. I cannot live without them. *Ahimsa* is my religion

—*Wit and Wisdom of Mahatma Gandhi,* p. 199

Practice

An ounce of practice is more than tons of preaching.

—*Wit and Wisdom of Mahatma Gandhi,* p. 217

Prayer

Prayer is a confession of one's own unworthiness and weakness. It is the key of the morning and bolt of the evening. Prayer accompanied by adequate suffering is prayer of the heart. Words without faith and prayer are like artificial flowers without fragrance. It is a bath of purification for the spirit of man.

Religion

Religion deals with the science of the soul. Great as the other forces of the world are, if there is such a thing as God, soul-force is the greatest of all. We know as a matter of fact that the greater the force the finer it is. Hitherto electricity has held the field among the finer physical powers. And yet nobody has seen it except through its wonderful results. Scientific speculation dares to talk of a force finer even than that of electricity. But no instrument devised by man has been able to know anything positive of soul-force or spiritual force. It is on that force that the true religious reformer has hitherto relied.

Religion is a matter of life and death. A man does not change religion as he changes his garments. He takes it with him beyond the grave.

—*Wit and Wisdom of Mahatma Gandhi,* N.B. Sen, p. 244

My religion says that only he who is prepared to suffer can pray to God. Fasting and prayer are common injunctions in my religion. But I know that there is a sort of penance even in Islam. In the life of the Prophet I have read that the Prophet often fasted and prayed, and forbade others to copy him. Someone asked him why he did not allow others to do the thing he himself was doing. "Because I live on food divine," he said. He achieved most of his great things by fasting and prayers. I learnt from him that only he can fast who has inexhaustible faith in God. The Prophet had revelations not in moments of ease and luxurious living. He fasted and prayed, kept awake for nights together and would be on his feet at all hours of the night as he received the revelations.

—*Wit and Wisdom of Mahatma Gandhi,* N.B. Sen

4

Bernard Shaw and Churchill

- A reporter was interviewing Sir Winston Churchill. "What do you say, Sir," he asked, "to the prediction that in the year 2000, women will be ruling the world?"

Churchill smiled his wise old cherub smile, "They still will, eh?"

—J.M. Braude, *Wit and Humour*

- Sir Winston Churchill, whose fondness for drink was well known, was scheduled to make a speech before a small gathering.

The chairman introduced him by saying: "If all the spirits consumed by Sir Winston were poured into this room, it would reach up to here on the wall."

He drew a line with his finger at about level with his eyes.

Churchill got up to speak. He glanced at the imaginary line on the wall. He looked up at the ceiling and made a mathematical calculation with his fingers. Then he sighed and said, "Ah, so much to be done, and so little time in which to do it."

—J.M. Braude, *Wit and Humour*

- Churchill once met General Montgomery and found him quite fit, hale and hearty. He asked the General what was the secret of his health. The General referred, "I get up early in the morning and do my exercise regularly. I don't smoke, don't drink. After my dinner I take regular walk for a mile or two. I go to bed early. I am hundred per cent fit."

Now Churchill started telling him, "General, I get up late in the morning. I never do any exercise, I smoke and drink heavily.

After dinner I don't go on walk, and I go to bed quite late. I am two hundred per cent fit."

• G.K. Chesterton and G.B. Shaw were good friends. While Chesterton was short and fat, Shaw was lean and thin and tall.

Once both were walking together in a London Street. People looked at them curiously. Chesterton remarked to Shaw, "Looking at you people must be thinking a famine has come to England." "Looking at you they would know whom to blame", remarked Shaw.

• At a gathering, a lady rebuked Churchill by saying, "Mr. Churchill, your politics is as awkward as your moustache." Do not distress yourself, lady", said Churchill," You are not likely to come in contact with either."

• Bernard Shaw happened to meet a famous authoress and formally greeted her, telling her that he was greatly happy to meet her. The lady regreted that she could not use the same greeting sentence for him. Bernard Shaw responded readily, "Respected madam! Can't you tell a lie like me to please someone's heart?"

—*From Hind Samachar,* Article by Nanakchand Journalist

• Bernard Shaw whenever accompanied his wife for shopping he would make purchases of his own liking. On the complaint of his wife he would silence her by saying that she did not know how to buy things of standard quality.

One day his wife got tired of listening to the same old cliché told Bernard Shaw, it appeared she had never made any good selection in her life.

Bernard Shaw retorted, no, that is not the case, once in life she did it. Her selection at the time of marriage was better than his.

A man is like a phonograph with half a dozen records. You soon get tired of them and yes you have to sit at the table whilst he reels them off to every new visitor.

—*George Bernard Shaw* (*Cutting Remarks* by Maria Leach, p. 25)

- Heaven as conventionally conceived is a place, so dull, so useless, so miserable, that nobody has ever ventured to describe a whole day in heaven, though plenty of people have described a day at the sea side.

—*George Bernard Shaw* (*Cutting Remarks* by Maria Leach, p. 37)

- George Bernard Shaw was discussing with his friend that he wanted to do something to impress his personality on the public. On being questioned what he intended to do, Shaw replied he wanted to start a magazine. He was put another question: what could be the title of magazine? Shaw's reply was Shaw Magazine. Oscar laughed and said 'Shah, Shah and Shah' but how would he spell it. All present laughed together.

—James Sutherland, *The Oxford Book of Literary Anecdotes,* p. 303

- During the Second World War British Prime Minister Mr. Churchill was to go to Radio Station to broadcast his speech. He hired one taxi and requested the driver to reach Radio Station at the earliest.

During dialogue Churchill inquired of the driver to know where he would go after dropping him at the Radio Station. The driver replied, "I have to reach home quickly to listen to my beloved leader Churchill on the radio."

While alighting from the taxi Churchill paid him handsome amount of 60 pounds and asked him to go home to hear his beloved leader Churchill. The driver was very happy and replied, "Damn with Churchill, please tell me when are you going back."

—From *Urdu Daily, Hind Samachar,* 27th February, 2007, Writer Madan Gopal Nagina, Amritsar

- "It is impossible to obtain a conviction for sodomy from an English Jury. Half of them don't believe that it ought physically be done, and the other half are doing it."

—Winston Churchill, *Delhi Times—What is hot—* 3.11.06, p. 22.

5

Generals and other Bigwigs

Mumbai: In the halfway of the National Centre of Performing Arts, close to where land meets sea, the excitement was palpable. The captains of Indian industry—the biggest and most influential—were all there, to salute the best among them at the 2006 edition of *The Economic Times Award.*

P. Chidambaram evoked the loudest applause for his sharp one liners that had the audience in splits. Accepting the award for business reformer of the year, he said: "But I haven't reformed any businessman. They continue to either avoid or evade taxes."

Subsequent to the PM's speech, he fielded questions from the audience. Responding to a question by Anand Mahindra, Vice Chairman, Mahindra & Mahindra on what the economy will look like 15 years from now, the PM joked there is no way he would know. Because he isn't an astrologer.

C. Rangarajan, perhaps described the early 90s' shift the best. As the Reserve Bank Governor Rangarajan had then just set about repairing the country's obsolete financial structure. "It was a new turn and direction in economic policy and management. It was like the birth of a child. It was painful," he said.

Those labour pains did deliver—most of all a new crop of uninhibited entrepreneurs.

—Wisdom, *Times of India,* 9.10.06, p. 16

Jurisdiction

Asked to officiate at a friend's wedding ceremony, Justice Felix Frankfurter explained that he did not have the authority to perform the ceremony.

"What!" exclaimed his friend. "A Supreme Court Justice doesn't have the authority to marry people! How come?"

"I guess," replied Frankfurter, "It is because marriage is not considered a federal offense."

—J.M. Braude, *Wit and Humour*

General Grant was brilliant enough to conquer Lee, win the Civil War, and became President of the United States; but he wasn't smart enough to keep out of Wall Street. During the last years of his life, two sharpers got hold of Grant, and persuaded him to go into business with them. Then these men used Grant's good name to manipulate all sorts of crooked deals. These men flim-flammed the public out of sixteen million dollars. When the crash came, Grant, in order to pay his debts, handed over his farm, his houses in Philadelphia and New York, and even the swords and trophies that had been presented to him.

He didn't have a dollar, and he was dying of cancer. He realized that when he was dead, his widow would be poverty-stricken. So, in order to provide for her, he decided to write his memoirs. He dictated until the cancer in his throat got so bad he couldn't speak. Then he finished the book with a pencil—finished it while he was suffering agony. He wrote the last chapter only three days before he died. Mark Twain published the book, and paid Mrs. Grant almost half a million dollars in royalty.

—Dale Carnegie, *Little Known Facts about Greatmen*

- The second largest university in the world is a Mohammedan College in Cairo, Egypt. The entrance examination to this University requires every student to repeat the Koran from memory. The Koran, which is the Mohammedan Bible, is almost as long as the New Testament, and three days required to recite it. Yet, everyone of more than twenty thousand students regularly accomplish that feat.

- Lord Byron boasted that he could repeat all the verses that he ever wrote; but Sir Walter Scott, on the other hand, had a very poor memory. He once praised one of his own poems very highly, thinking that Byron had written it.
- Lord Bacon was able to dictate one of his most famous books from memory; but Joseph Jefferson, on the other hand, played "Rip Van Winkle" almost every night for a dozen years and kept forgetting his lines right up to the very end.

—Dale Carnegie, *Little Known Facts about Greatmen*

An American GI who met Pablo Picasso in Paris told the artist that he didn't like modern paintings because they weren't realistic. Picasso made no immediate reply. A few minutes later the soldier showed him a snapshot of his girl friend.

"My word," said Picasso, "is she really as small as all that?"

—J.M. Braude, *Wit and Humour*

An Englishman, a Welshman and a Scotsman were left legacies by a friend on condition that each should put five pounds in his coffin.

The Englishman put in a five-pound note. The Welshman also put in five pounds which he had borrowed from the Englishman.

The Scotsman took out the two five-pound notes and put in a cheque for fifteen pounds, payable to bearer.

Three days later he was astonished to learn that the cheque had been presented and encashed. The undertaker was an Irishman.

—J.M. Braude, *Wit and Humour*

A pompous gentleman once asked the sharp-tongued actress, Mrs. Patrick Campbell, "Why do you suppose it is that women so utterly lack a sense of humour?"

"God did it on purpose," Mrs. Campbell answered without batting an eyelash, "so that we then may love you instead of laughing at you." —J.M. Braude, *Wit and Humour*

Justice

To a recently arrived immigrant the processes of law and order were baffling. He had the misfortune to be arrested for peddling without a licence. Now he stood before the bar of justice with three young ladies arrested for soliciting. When the first young lady gave her profession as "actress" the judge sentenced her to thirty days in the workhouse. When the second said she was "a model" she drew a sixty-day sentence.

"And what do you do for a living?" the judge fired at the third girl.

"To tell you the truth, your honour," she answered. "I'm a prostitute."

Taken aback by this burst of frankness the judge said, "Honesty has become such a rare commodity in these parts that for telling the truth I'm suspending sentence. You are free to go." Then he turned to the peddler, his face hardened. "And what do you do for a living?"

"To tell you the truth, judge," he replied, "I'm a prostitute also."

—J.M. Braude, *Wit and Humour*

Alexander H.H. Stuart and Daniel Webster were both members of President Fillmore's cabinet. One day, on coming home, Stuart found in his hall a brace of ducks with Mr. Webster's name on them.

Knowing they were left by mistake, he told his coachman to take them to Webster's house and tell him the facts. In time the coachman returned with the ducks.

"I have delivered your message to Mr. Webster," said the coachman. "I told him the ducks were left at your house by mistake."

"What did he say?" asked the puzzled Stuart.

"Well, sir," replied the coachman, "Mr. Webster told me to take the ducks back to you and thank you for being more honest than he is for your ducks, which were left at his house by mistake, and are already on the fire."

—J.M. Braude, *Wit and Humour*

Adolf Hitler was very much disturbed when a clairvoyant let it be known that she could predict the exact day of the Fuhrer's death. Since her predictions were always based on astrology, and since Hitler himself was a believer in the stars, he sent for the woman. After much divination the woman finally said that the omens indicated no specific date for the passing of the Nazi leader, other than that it would definitely take place on a Jewish holiday.

"Which holiday" Hitler demanded.

"I cannot be sure," said the astrologist.

"You've got to be sure," Hitler ordered, going off into one of his spastic shrieks. "I demand that you be sure."

"What difference does it make?" shrugged the woman. "Any day on which you die will be a Jewish holiday?"

—J.M. Braude, *Wit and Humour*

It's better to help others get on than to tell them where to get off.

Heywood Brown, the New York newspaperman, was leaving the theatre after a Broadway opening and met the producer in the lobby. The latter took one look at Brown's suit, which was rumpled as usual, and said with some annoyance:

"That's a fine way to dress for my opening. Your suit looks as if it had been slept in."

"Since you mention it", replied Brown, "I just woke up."

—J.M. Braude, *Wit and Humour*

Lord North, Premier of Britain, lost his heart to a beautiful actress who did not like him. Lord North was ugly, and was rejected by her whenever he approached her. He one day went to her and told her that he loved her greatly. He asked her why she did not like him, what was wrong with him? Having been exasperated with his constant wooing, she replied suddenly, "your face".

—*Hind Samachar,* Journalist Nanak Chand

One stormy night, Frank Lloyd Wright, noted Wisconsin architect, was roused from a sound sleep by an urgent phone call from a client who had just moved into his Wright built house.

"There's a leak in the roof and the living room is flooded," cried the man. "What shall I do?"

Advised Wright, "Rise above it."

—J.M. Braude, *Wit and Humour*

When President Teddy Roosevelt was touring Oklahoma, he drove by to see his old friend, Quanah Parker, Chief of the Comanches, who lived 12 miles from Fort Sill. With pride Parker showed Teddy the house he lived in, the whiteman's clothes he wore and his children who attended the whiteman's school.

"See here, Chief," Teddy said, "why don't you set your people a still better example of obeying the laws of the land and the customs of the whites? A whiteman has only one wife, and here you are living with five squaws. Why don't you give up four of them and remain faithful to the fifth? Then you would really be living as the whiteman lives."

Parker considered the proposition. "You are my great white father," he said, "and I will do as you wish on one condition."

"You pick out the one I am to live with—and then you go tell the other four."

—J.M. Braude, *Wit and Humour*

Novelist Sinclair Lewis was to lecture a group of college students who planned literary careers. Lewis opened his talk by saying:

"How many of you really intend to be writers?"

All hands went up.

"In that case," said Lewis, returning his notes to his pocket, "my advice to you is to go home and write."

With that, he left the room.

—J.M. Braude, *Wit and Humour*

Heywood Broun hated ghost-written political speeches. His comment was that usually they failed to reflect the personality or the convictions of the individuals who delivered them.

It was during a newsmen's dinner that President Harding delivered a real Websteronian oration loaded with outlandish clichés and pompous language. It was completely out of character. As the polite applause died down after the President had finished, Broun leaped from his seat and cried:

"Author! Author!"

—J.M. Braude, *Wit and Humour*

George Washington Carver, Negro scientist who achieved wonders with the humble peanut, used to tell this story:

When I was young I said to God, "God, tell me the mystery of the universe." But God answered, "That knowledge is reserved for Me alone." So I said, "God tell me the mystery of the Peanut." Then God said, "Well, George, that's more nearly your size." And He told me.

—J.M. Braude, *Wit and Humour*

Joseph H. Choate, one-time ambassador to Great Britain, was

called upon at a dinner of the Pilgrim Fathers to respond to the toast, "The Pilgrim Fathers."

After paying tribute to the Pilgrim Fathers for enduring the rigours of the New England winters and the privations and dangers of life in the little settlement of Plymouth, he paused.

"But let us give thought," he added with a grin, "to the Pilgrim Mothers. For they not only had to endure everything the Pilgrim Fathers endured, but mark this they had to endure, also, the Pilgrim Fathers."

• Once when J. Sterling Morton was making a speech, a man in the crowd shouted, "Louder!" Mr. Morton raised his voice which was always more sonorous than a whisper, but the man yelled "Louder!" again.

Mr. Morton once more put on steam, and his voice stretched out to the edges of the crowd as he lambasted the free silver apostasy of his well known political enemy, William Jennings Bryan.

—J.M. Braude, *Wit and Humour*

• Following the famous compensation bill, Henry Clay found a formidable opposition arrayed against him for re-election. After addressing a crowd, he was stepping down from the platform to mingle with the voters when he was approached by an old friend named Scott—a great huntsman in the district.

"Well, Henry," said Scott, "I've been with you in six troubles, and I'm sorry I must desert you in the seventh. You voted for that miserable compensation bill and now I must turn my back on you."

"Is that your only objection?" asked Clay.

"It is."

"You are an old huntsman," said Clay, "and have killed many a fat bear and buck?"

"Yes," said Scott.

"I believe you have a good rifle?" continued Clay.

"Yes, as good a one as ever cracked."

"Well, then", smiled Clay, "did you ever have a fine buck before you when your gun misfired?"

"Yes, that has happened."

"Well, now friend Scott, did you take that faithful rifle and break it to pieces on the very next log just because it misfired once, or did you pick the flint and try again?"

"No, Mr. Clay," laughed Scott. "I picked the flint and tried again. And I'll try you again. Give me your hand." The crowd also got the point, the story spread and Clay was re-elected.

—J.M. Braude, *Wit and Humour*

● Like every other president, William Howard Taft had to endure his share of abuse. One night at the dinner table his youngest boy made a disrespectful remark to him. There was a sudden hush. Taft became thoughtful.

"Well," said Mrs. Taft, "aren't you going to punish him?"

"If the remark was addressed to me as his father he certainly will be punished," said Taft. "However, if he addressed it to the President of the United States, that is his Constitutional privilege."

—J.M. Braude, *Wit and Humour*

● George Washington had been visiting the home of friends and the hour came for him to leave. After saying goodbye to the adults, he paused at the entrance where a little girl opened the door to let him out.

Washington bowed to her and said, "I am sorry, my little dear, to give you so much trouble."

She replied, "I wish, sir, it was to let you in."

—J.M. Braude, *Wit and Humour*

• Sir Herbert Beerbohm Tree, British actor and manager, once berated a young actor for his over bearing conceit.

"I assure you, sir," said the other indignantly, "that I am not suffering from a swelled head."

"It isn't the swelling that causes suffering," retorted Tree. "It's the subsequent shrinkage that hurts."

—J.M. Braude, *Wit and Humour*

Ranjit Singh was not only intellectually curious and inquisitive, he was remarkably humane at a time when India and the world seethed with callousness and inhumanity. He built up a kingdom and a powerful army and yet he disliked bloodshed. 'Never was so large an empire founded by one man with so little criminality,' says Prinsep. He abolished the death sentence for every crime, however heinous it might be, when in England even petty pilferers had to face death. 'Except in actual warfare', writes Osborne, who visited him, 'he was never been known to take life, though his own has been attempted more than once, and his reign will be found free from any striking acts of cruelty and oppression than those of many more civilized monarches.'

—Jawaharlal Nehru, *Discovery of India,* p. 283

During the Mughal period large numbers of Hindus wrote books in Persian which was the official court language. Some of these books have become classics of their kind. At the same time Muslim scholars translated Sanskrit books into Persian and wrote in Hindi. Two of the best-known Hindi poets are Malik Mohammad Jaisi who wrote the 'Padmavat' and Abdul Rahim Khankhana, one of the premier nobles of Akbar's court and son of his guardian. Khankhana was a scholar in Arabic, Persian, and Sanskrit, and his Hindi poetry is of a high quality. For sometime he was the commander-in-chief of the imperial army, and yet he has written in praise and admiration of Rana Pratap of Mewar, who was continually fighting Akbar and never submitted to him. Khankhana admires and commends the patriotism and high sense of honour and chivalry of his enemy on the battlefield.

—Jawaharlal Nehru, *Discovery of India,* p. 269

The Turks were also fine horsemen, and the love of the Arab for his horse is well-known. In north and west India there are some good breeding-grounds for horses, especially in Kathiawar, and the Rajputs are very fond of their horses. Many a petty war was waged for a famous charger. There is a story of a Delhi Sultan admiring the charger of a Rajput chief and asking him for it. The Hara chief replied to the Lodi king: 'There are three things you must not ask of a Rajput: his mistress, his charger, or his sword,' and he galloped away. There was trouble afterwards.

—Jawaharlal Nehru, *Discovery of India,* p. 239

Henry Ward Beecher, famous New England clergyman, was opening his mail one morning. Drawing a single sheet of paper from an envelope, he found written on it the one word: Fool.

The next Sunday, in the course of his sermon, he referred to it in these words: "I have known many an instance of a man writing letters and forgetting to sign his name. But this is the only instance I've ever known of a man signing his name and forgetting to write his letter."

—J.M. Braude, *Wit and Humour*

Parson Webster phoned the local board of health to ask that a dead mule be removed from the front of his house. The young clerk who answered thought he'd be smart.

"I thought your ministers took care of the dead", he wisecracked.

"We do," answered the Parson, "but first we get in touch with their relatives."

—J.M. Braude, *Wit and Humour*

The millionaire speculator, John W. (Bet-a-Million) Gates was a lavish tipper. Ironically, this resulted at times in poorer service.

Gates was a particular favourite of bellhops. At one time, when he was stopping at a New York hotel, he instructed his secretary to tip them 25c for any service, no matter how trivial.

After a few weeks, it struck him that he must be getting a staggering amount of service, as the tips were running into several hundred dollars a week. His heavy mail, about 100 letters a day, was being brought up with something less than promptness.

Gates put two and two together and made an investigation. Sure enough, he discovered that the mail was being delivered one letter at a time.

—J.M. Braude, *Wit and Humour*

Tact

When a prominent cleargyman was asked his opinion of advertising in America, he hesitated to make any comment on advertising itself, but he did offer to pray for the people who made a living at it.

George Clemenceau, noted French statesman, was in the habit of bluntly speaking his mind, to the dismay of his political advisers.

"You must be more tactful", they urged him. "Your strong language only makes you enemies."

Clemenceau couldn't see it that way.

"It also makes me friends," he argued. "I have as my supporters all the enemies of my enemies."

—J.M. Braude, *Wit and Humour*

Chengiz Khan was not a Muslim, as some people seem to imagine because of his name which is now associated with Islam.

He is said to have believea in Shamaism, a religion of the sky. What this was I do not know but the word inevitably makes one think of the Arab word for Buddhists—Samani, which was derived from the Sanskrit Shravana. Debased forms of Buddhism flourished then in various parts of Asia, including Mongolia and it is probable that Chengiz grew up under their influence.

It is odd to think that the greatest military conqueror in history was probably some kind of a Buddhist.

—Jawaharlal Nehru, *Discovery of India*, p. 231

Thousands of people have had remarkable memories. Theodore Roosevelt was one of them. He was intensely interested in meeting people. He found out little personal details about the people he met, studied their faces, their mannerism, and repeated their names until they were indelibly impressed upon his memory. This helped him enormously in his political life. He made people feel immensely important by calling their names the second time he met them.

—Dale Carnegie, *Little Known Facts About Well-known People*

Lord Welseley writes in the *Soldier's Pocket-Book for Field Service:* "We will keep hammering along with the conviction that 'honesty is the best policy', and that truth always wins in the long run. These pretty sentences do well for a child's copy-book, but the man who acts upon them in war had better sheathe his sword for ever."

—Jawaharlal Nehru, *An Autobiography*, p. 269

When Gladstone was managing the affairs of England for Queen Victoria, he had four desks in his office—one for literary work, one for correspondence, one for political affairs and one for his favourite studies. Gladstone found he could work better when he got variety; so he would work awhile at one desk and then move to another.

—Dale Carnegie, Little Known Facts About Well-known People

Once, when William Gladstone was Britain's Chancellor of the Exchequer, he attended a lecture given by Michael Faraday, the physicist. When it was over, Gladstone said to the scientist: "What you spoke about is purely theoretical, but does it have any practical value?"

"What do you mean by 'practical value'?" asked Faraday.

"I mean", replied Gladstone, "can it be taxed?"

— J.M. Braude, *Wit and Humour*

In his youth the American sculptor Gutzon Borglum studied art in Paris. Like most students he had a hard time making ends meet. When winter came, his studio was bitterly cold, but since he was unable to buy fuel, he had to rely on his imagination to keep him warm.

He would place a lighted candle in the stove and cover the door with a strip of red sun glass. The rosy glow gave such an illusion of warmth that he was able to continue his work without too much discomfort.

— J.M. Braude, *Wit and Humour*

Artist Pablo Picasso surprised a burglar at work in his new chateau. The intruder got away, but Picasso told the police he could do a rough sketch of what he looked like. On the basis of his drawing, the police arrested a mother superior, the minister of finance, a washing machine, and the Eiffel tower.

— J.M. Braude, *Wit and Humour*

Mrs. Ronnie Greville once gave a cocktail party for about thirty guests, including Sir Austen Chamberlain, then foreign secretary, and his wife.

Mrs. Greville's Butler was obviously not quiet herself. Reluctant to make a scene, she handed him a note which said: "Leave the room at once. You are drunk."

This analysis was evidently accurate. The Butler promptly handed the note, on a salver, to Lady Chamberlain.

—J.M. Braude, *Wit and Humour*

- Narendra Jadhav, leading economist and author, Chief Economist of the Reserve Bank of India—His father was once asked why he did not follow Gandhi who was the chief patron of Harijans. Why he followed Ambedkar. He replied that he followed Ambedker as he was a Dalit. He did not like the word Harijan coined by Gandhiji. "If Harijans are the people of God, who are the other people? devils?"

—*Readers' Digest*, October, 2006, p. 117

- In 1936, Dr. Ambedkar convinced that the upper castes would never treat Dalits fairly, he announced that although he was born a Hindu, he was not going to die as one. For 20 years he pondered alternatives and finally, settled on Buddhism—because it was an Indian religion, unlike Islam and Christianity.

—*Reader Digest*, October, 2006, p. 118

- In America only the successful writer is important, in France all writers are important, and in Australia you have to explain what a writer is.

—Maria Leach, *Cutting Remarks,* p. 17

Lord Nelson was besotted with a prostitute

- He helped England to rule the waves with his sense of discipline and duty. But newly published letters reveal how Lord Nelson was overwhelmed by passion of his mistress.

She was a former prostitute who rose to become a diplomat's wife.

In January 1799, a few months after their affair had begun, Nelson wrote his lover that he had awoken "twenty times in the night" thinking of her. He said that during one of his dreams he was sitting between two women, including a princess.

He wrote: "They both tried to seduce me and the first wanted to take those liberties with me which no woman in the world but yourself ever did, the consequence was I knocked her down and in the moment of bustle you came in and taking me to your embrace whispered (*sic*) I love nothing but you my Nelson, I kissed you fervently and we enjoy'd the height of love."

He writes: "What must be my sensations at the idea of sleeping with you! It sets me on fire, even the thoughts, much more would be reality. I am sure love and desires are all to you, and if any woman naked were to come to me, even as I am at this moment from thinking of you, I hope it might rot off if I would touch her even with my hand."

—Richard Brooks, *Sunday Times,* London, 2-10-2006

- During the rainy season, Ghalib happened to meet one of his friends who knew that roof of Ghalib's room leaked. He asked Ghalib about the leakage of the latter's room. Ghalib in his humorous way replied as under "It rains outside for an hour but it rains two hours in my room".

- Some one learnt that there was some one in Ghalib's family who died yesterday. He came for the mourning, but before mourning he asked Ghalib who in his family died yesterday.

  Ghalib in his light tone replied that all his relatives died yesterday. The gentleman on hearing this stood flabbergasted. Ghalib looking at him started clarifying. "Yesterday my auntie who was living with me died. As long as she was alive I had forgotten all my dead relatives. On her death I remembered all of them and felt that all died yesterday along with her."

• After the war of independence, 1857, living in Delhi became very costly. The royal poet of the time, Zauq met the famous Urdu poet Ghalib and advised him to leave Delhi. Ghalib in his own pleasant way replied in the following verse:

"*Kaun Jāē Ghālib Dilli Ki Galiān Chhor Kar*" (Who would like to leave the streets of Delhi).

Zauq immediately responded in his own verse:

"*Ye mānā ki Dilli mein rahaein khaeinge kya*" (Admitted we should stay in Delhi but what would we eat?)

• Dr. Rahim a distinguished biologist from Switzerland, was speaking on religion on Nandi Hill near Bangalore, in May 1936, Sir C.V. Raman interrupted him.

Sir C.V. Raman: "Pardon me, for the interruption. If there is God, we must look for him in the Universe. If he is not there, he is not worth looking for. I am being looked upon as atheist but I am not. The growing discoveries in Science offer the best opportunity for a complete fellowship. All men of science are brothers."

Mahatma Gandhi: "But what about the converse? All who are not men of science are not brothers?"

Sir C.V. Raman: "But all can become men of science."

Mahatma Gandhi: "You will have to present a *Kalma* of science as Islam presents one."

• A conversation between Sir C.V. Raman and Ravi Yogi Maharshi.

The spiritualist remarked: "Raman's effect on the scientific world".

Dr. Raman showed a beautiful car and asked whether he wanted to see God seated in it.

After listening "Yes", he suddenly produced a crystal and passed a dazzling light through it. There was a splendid light on the seat of the car. Raman danced with joy and declared— "Behold God, the luminous science".

He believed all artists and scientists of light must bow to the smile of flowers. In the decent stone and cement building of Raman, there was a grand simplicity.

Raman's Research Institute established in eleven acres pulsates with his heart and brain every inch. That tall imposing figure is no more, but his soul is there inspiring us to go deeper into the realm of modern science.

• At the prize awarding ceremony in Stockholm, Raman demonstrated the "Effect" using a number of liquids, one of them was alcohol. The desk drew near and the stage was set for a grand cocktail reception to the Nobel laureate. "This morning Raman demonstrated his effect on alcohol. Now we would see the "alcohol's effect on Raman" an invitee cracked pushing a glass in Raman's direction. The reaction was not reversible, the effect was not reciprocal, with a modest "thanks" the glass was returned, for Raman was a teetotaller.

• Once some foreign scientists visited Raman Research Institute and Sir C.V. Raman remarked if they wanted to see a 'photon'. They said, "Yes" in front of the world famous scientist; though they knew that a photon could not be singled out. Dr. Raman had an arrangement of slits whose widths can be decreased progressively. He operated the widest slit and said, "See the beam of light entering". He decreased the width and said, "Look, the beam is becoming narrow". He went on decreasing the width of the slits and when it became the smallest, he remarked, "Look at the photon entering the room". The visitors nodded their heads in agreement.

Emperor Aurangzeb followed strictly the tenets of Islam. His life was the life of a Muslim puritan. One day he issued a decree to ban music and dance, demanded strict observance of the law.

The musicians found themselves in great trouble. Some of them were sure to lose their jobs. The Emperor was requested to have mercy on them. When nothing happened they thought of preparing a funeral procession and go before the Red Fort when the Emperor came for a walk on the rampart. They did it, the Emperor was walking on the rampart and saw a funeral procession below. He asked his bodyguard who had died. He was at once told that music had died. He sent down the bodyguard to instruct them to bury the dead so deep that it would be impossible for him to come up.

- Zaibul-nisa, daughter of Aurangzeb was liberal in her views. She liked music and dancing. One day she was sitting beside her father near the window. Suddenly a Nightingale came and sat on the nearby tree. It began to sing in her mellifluous voice.

Zaibul-nisa in her taunting tone addressed the bird. "Oh sweet bird! Why are you singing here in the presence of our Emperor who has a very delicate temperament. He does not like music so he has banned it. Perhaps you don't know this. Now you know it, so fly away, otherwise he will punish you."

Emperor at once understood those remarks were meant for him, but he felt helpless before a small bird.

6

Albert Einstein

Believe it or not Albert Einstein's first academic paper was on the physics of drinking straws.

Times of India, 25-10-2006

His teachers despaired; he even learned to talk with difficulty.

Einstein had a characteristic which every true scientist must possess—unbounded curiosity. One day, he heard the word 'ALGEBRA'. It was a curious word for him, so he asked his uncle what it meant.

His uncle replied that Algebra was a lazy man's arithmetic. If you do not know a thing, call it X and act as if you do know it.

Einstein had a keen sense of humour, something not quite common to great scientists.

The young Einstein, before he became world famous for his Theory of Relativity, was one day taking part in a symposium in a certain university. The discussions bored him and he slipped away into a restaurant on the other side of the road. The boy greeted him and held out the menu before him. The young professor searched his pockets for his spectacles but remembered that he had forgotten them on the symposium dais.

"Will you please read out the menu to me?" He asked the boy. The boy looked at him with sympathy and whispered, "I *too* am as illiterate as you are".

- When Einstein visited USA for the first time in April 1921, he was surrounded by the Press people as soon as the ship arrived at the port. They shot various questions at him.

Q. Can you explain the theory of relativity in one sentence?
A. No.
Q. How many people in the world can understand your theory?
A. Any physicist who studies it.

- When Einstein reached his fiftieth birthday, Germany overwhelmed him with honours, erected a bust of him at Potsdam, and offered him a home and a sail boat as a token of the nation's love and undying admiration.

But, a few years later, his property had been taken away from him and he was afraid to return to his native land. For weeks he lived in Belgium behind barred doors and a policeman slept at his bedside every night.

- When he arrived in New York to become Professor of Mathematics in the Institute for Advanced Study at Princeton, he was anxious to avoid reporters and interviews and excitement: so his friends took him off the ship secretly before it docked and hurried him away by automobile.

Einstein says that there are only twelve people living who understand his Theory of Relativity, although more than nine hundred books have been written attempting to explain it.

He himself explains Relativity by this very simple illustration: when you sit with a nice girl for an hour, you think it is only a minute; but when you sit on a hot stove for a minute, you think it is an hour.

Well, well—so that's relativity. It sounds all right to me; but if you doubt it, try it out. I'll be glad to sit with the girl not on the stove.

And speaking of girls, Einstein has been married twice. He has two boys by his first marriage, both brilliant chaps with the earmarks of genius.

—Dale Carnegie, *Little Known Facts About Well-known People*

- A. (smilingly) Because women like a fashion every year and this year it is the fashion to be interested in relativity, she again asked him to tell her about relativity.

He said, Madam, I was once walking with a blind friend in the country side on a hot, dry day and said, 'I should like a drink of milk.'

'Milk,' said my friend, 'what is milk?'

'A white liquor', I said.

'Liquor, I know, but what is white?' said the blind man.

'The colour of a swan's feathers' I told him.

'Feather I know, but what is Swan?'

'Swan is a bird with a crooked neck.'

'Neck I know, but what is crooked?'

Thereupon I lost my patience, seized his arm and straightened it.

'That is straight,' I said.

Then I bent it at the elbow and said that is crooked.

'Ah!' cried the blind man.

'Now I understand what you mean by milk.'

- Professor Berganann, a co-worker of Einstein while delivering inaugural speech of the Arthur Eddington centennial symposium at Nagpur related that after enunciating the General Theory of Relativity Einstein had said, "If my theory proves correct, Germans will call me a German scientist and the British will call me a world scientist. If it fails, Germans will brand me a Jew and British will call me a German scientist."

Little Known Facts

Mrs. Einstein admits that even she doesn't understand the Theory of Relativity; but she understands something that is far more important for a wife; she understands her husband.

She used to invite her friends in for tea occasionally and then she would ask the Professor to come downstairs and join them. "No!" he would exclaim violently. "No! *I won't! I won't!* I'm going away from here. I can't work here. I simply won't stand these interruptions any longer."

Frau Einstein would keep perfectly quiet until he had blown off steam for a while; and then, presently, by using a little diplomacy, she would have him downstairs drinking tea and getting some much-needed relaxation.

Frau Einstein says that her husband likes order in his thinking, but he doesn't like it in his living. He does whatever he wants to, whenever he wants to. And he has only two rules of conduct. The first one is: Don't have any rules whatever. And the second one is: Be independent of the opinions of others.

He leads a very simple sort of an existence, goes around in old clothes that need pressing, seldom wears a hat, and whistles and sings in the bathroom. He shaves while sitting in the bath tub and doesn't use shaving soap. He shaves with the same soap that he uses for his bath. This man who is trying to solve the vexing riddles of the universe says that using two kinds of soap makes life entirely too complicated. Einstein impresses me as being a very happy man. His philosophy of happiness means far more to me than does his Theory of Relativity. I think it a splendid philosophy. He says he is happy because he doesn't want anything from anybody. He doesn't want money or titles or praise. He makes his own happiness out of such simple things as his work and playing the violin and sailing his boat.

Einstein's violin brings him more joy than anything else in life. He says he often thinks in music and lives his day dreams in music.

Once, while riding a street car in Berlin, he told the conductor that he hadn't given him the right change. The conductor counted the change again and found it to be correct, so he handed it back to Einstein saying: "The trouble with you is, you don't know figures."

***

The captain of a Transatlantic ship once offered Einstein the most expensive suite of rooms on the vessel; but Einstein declined and said he would rather travel in the steerage than accepting any special favours.

***

Germany's late Cardinal von Faulhaber of Munich once had a conversation with the renowned mathematician, Albert Einstein.

"Cardinal von Faulhaber," Einstein remarked. "I respect religion, but I believe in mathematics. Probably it is the other way around with you."

"You are mistaken," the Cardinal retorted. "To me, both are merely different expressions of the same divine exactness."

"But, Your Eminence, what would you say if mathematical science should someday come to conclusions, directly contradictory to religious beliefs?"

"Oh," answered the Cardinal, "I have the highest regard for the competence of mathematicians. I am sure they would never rest until they discovered their mistake."

—J.M. Braude, *Writ and Humour*

Einstein had to pay a heavy price for his divorce from his first wife Milera. He offered her a deal if she agreed to give him a divorce, he would give her the money from the Nobel Prize he fully expected to win someday. She considered the offer for a week, then took the bet. And when he won a few years later, she was paid and with that money she was able to buy three apartment buildings in Zurich.

—*Times,* 24-7-2006,

The Theory of Relativity

"The theory was one of history's most imaginative and dramatic revisions of our concepts about the universe", said Paul Dirac, the Nobel Laureate, Pioneer of Quantum Mechanics, "probably the greatest scientific discovery ever made".

Max Born, another giant of 20th century physics, called it, the greatest feat of human thinking about nature, the most amazing combination of philosophical penetration, physical institution and mathematical skill.

—*Times,* 24-7-2006,

Einstein Lover Uncovered

An obscure lover of Albert Einstein's has emerged in letters unsealed by the Hebrew University, shedding new light on the personal life of the 20th century's greatest intellect.

Ethel Michanowski, a Berlin socialite, was involved with Einstein in the late 1920s and early 30s—going so far as to chase him to England, said Barbara Wolff, an archivist at the university's Einstein Archives. She was a friend of Einstein's step-daughters and was about 30-15 years younger than Einstein—at the time of their affair, Wolff said.

More than 3,500 pages of correspondence were written between 1912 and 1955, the year Einstein died.

Among the revelations: Einstein lost much of his Nobel Prize money in the Great Depression, was a more devoted father than previously thought and made no bones about discussing his romantic liaisons with his second wife.

Einstein is known to have had 10 lovers, in addition to the two women he married after affairs with them.

—*Hindustan Times,* 11-7-2006

Einstein and XU

On a recent morning, Xu held forth from an armchair on his adventures as an Einsteinian democrat, jabbing the air, waving his arms and laughing often. Albert Einstein started down sternly from above a file cabinet. "Great spirits have always encountered violent opposition from mediocre minds," the inscription read. Clad in a blue shirt, slippers and thick glasses, Xu got up from his easy chair to stand beneath the poster: "Those are some of his best words", he said.

The love affair between Xu, who was born in Linhai, Zhejiang, in 1920, and Einstein began when Xu was in secondary school and read a collection of Einstein's essays called *The World as I See It.* The book had as much politics as science. In one passage that the young Xu underlined, Einstein wrote: "The state is made for man, not man for the state. I regard the chief duty of the state to protect the individual and give him the opportunity to develop into a creative personality." Xu said, "I wanted to be such a person." —*Hindustan Times,* 20-9-2006

- In spite of all his pressing engagements and other activities, Einstein had a sense of humour. Once a lady reporter asked him if he ever stopped thinking about physics and thought of something more interesting. Einstein remarked, "Of course, madam, but not with you."

To a student having trouble in studying maths at school he said, "Do not worry about your difficulties in Maths. Mine are still greater than yours."

When an eminent psychologist wrote and asked that he be allowed to analyse him, said Einstein, "I regret, because I would like very much to remain in the darkness of not having been analysed."

He was great and essentially a good man. One of his admirers said about him, "Before you meet Einstein, you look forward to the experience of talking to a great man and afterwards you experience that you have had a moving experience. You have seen and talked to a good and simple man."

A huge statue of Einstein was unveiled at the National Academy of Sciences, Washington. The base of the monument showed the position of 3000 stars on March 14, 1879 when the physicist was born.

Life Comes from a Beautiful Mind

A picture Sign hanging in Einstein's office at Princeton: Not everything that counts can be counted, and not everything that can be counted counts.

He would make a funny face like a child when the situation required.

***

Anger dwells only in the bosom of fools.

***

The tragedy of life is what dies inside a man while he lives.

***

People like us, who believe in physics, know that the

distinction between past, present, and future is only a stubbornly persistent illusion.

***

Gravitation is not responsible for people falling in love.

***

I want to know God's thoughts; the rest are details.

***

Sometimes one pays most for the things one gets for nothing.

***

Science without religion is lame. Religion without science is blind.

***

Anyone who has never made a mistake has never tried anything new.

***

There are two ways to live your life—one is as though nothing is a miracle, the other is as though everything is a miracle.

***

Everything should be made as simple as possible, but not simpler.

***

Common sense is the collection of prejudices acquired by age eighteen.

***

The only thing that interferes with my learning is my education.

***

God does not care about our mathematical difficulties. He integrates empirically.

***

The whole of science is nothing more than a refinement of everyday thinking.

***

Technological progress is like an axe in the hands of a pathological criminal.

***

We can't solve problems by using the same kind of thinking we used when we created them.

***

As far as the laws of mathematics refer to reality, they are not certain, as far as they are certain, they do not refer to reality.

***

The important thing is not to stop questioning. Curiosity has its own reason for existing.

***

If A is a success in life, then A equals x plus y plus z. Work is x; y is play; and z is keeping your mouth shut.

***

Two things are infinite, the universe and human stupidity; and I'm not sure about the universe.

***

Education is what remains after one has forgotten everything he learned in school.

***

Imagination is more important than knowledge.

***

How on earth are you ever going to explain in terms of chemistry and physics so important a biological phenomenon as first love?

***

Most teachers waste their time by asking questions which are intended to discover what a pupil does not know, whereas the true art of questioning has for its purpose to discover what the pupil knows or is capable of knowing.

***

The greatest scientists are always artists as well.

***

Humiliation and mental oppression by ignorant and selfish teachers wreak havoc in the youthful mind that can never be undone and often exert a harmful influence in later life.

***

Teaching should be such that what is offered is perceived as a valuable gift and not as a hard duty.

***

Equations are more important to me, because politics is for the present, but an equation is something for eternity.

***

Whoever undertakes to set himself up as a judge of Truth and Knowledge is shipwrecked by the laughter of the gods.

***

In order to form an immaculate member of a flock of sheep one must, above all, be a sheep.

***

Great spirits have always encountered violent opposition from mediocrities. The latter cannot understand it when a man does not thoughtlessly submit to hereditary prejudices—instead, he honestly and courageously uses his intelligence.

7

Some Other Dignitaries

ALEXANDER DUMAS

Alexander Dumas, the man who wrote *The Three Musketeers,* was one of the most astonishing novelists that ever dipped a goose quill into ink. He loved to boast that he had more than five hundred children. His estimate may have been a trifle optimistic; but in spite of his fat, grotesque appearance, he did have a way with women. He declared over and over again that he would never marry. But he boasted once too often and one of his sweethearts called his bluff. She had her guardian buy up all of Alexander's debts at a bargain price. In those days, you could be clamped into jail for debt; so Dumas, the great lover, was politely informed that he could take his choice—marry or go to the hoosegow. He married.

Dumas even *looked* strange. Three-fourths of the blood that coursed through his arteries was white; but the other fourth was negro. His grandmother had been a negro slave.

—Dale Carnegie, *Little Known Facts about Well Known People*

An epicure and a gourmet, he was nearly as famous for his ability to concoct a sauce or roast a duck as for his ability to write a novel. He would consume a meal of caviar, *pate de foie gras,* fish, filet mignon, roast partridge, half a dozen kind of vegetables, and top it off with vast quantities of cheese. He would eat a meal that would have put even Bismarck to shame; yet, in spite of his gluttonous appetite, he never drank liquor or coffee, and he never smoked. When he was busy writing, he didn't even care about food; and sometimes he even forgot to eat at all. If a friend dropped in to see him while he was working, he simply held out his left hand in greeting and kept on scribbling with his right hand.

But he was frightfully temperamental about the kind of paper and pens he used.

For example, he could only write novels on blue paper, and with a special set of pens. If he was writing poetry, he used yellow paper and a different set of pens. If he was writing an article for a magazine, he couldn't possibly use anything but rose-coloured writing paper; and he never, under any circumstances, used blue ink. Blue ink gave him the jitters. And he couldn't compose a play while sitting at his desk. In order to write a play, he had to lie down on a sofa with a good soft pillow propped under his elbow.

He didn't have time to read his own books; but he did have time to fight twenty duels with swords and pistols.

He didn't drink and he didn't sing; but he did go in for girls in a big way.

CHARLES DARWIN

While contemplating marriage Charles drew a list with columns headed "marry" and "not marry". Entries in pre-marriage column included "constant companion and friend in old age... better than a dog any how" and the ones listed against marriage were, "less money for books", and terrible loss of time. The pros won and he married his cousin Emma.

—*Times of India,* 29.11.2006, Under Heading, 'The Sign of Great Minds', p. 9 of Magazine Section

EDGAR ALLAN POE

Edgar Allan Poe was one of the most striking and romantic geniuses that ever wrote a sonnet or concocted a mystery. He was destined to stride like a melancholy giant across the pages of American literature. Yet he was removed from the University of Virginia because of his wild passion for gambling and drinking; and later on, he was court-martialled and kicked out of West Point because he ignored all rules and sat in his quarters writing poetry when he ought to have been out on the parade ground drilling with a gun.

Poe was left an orphan early in life, and adopted by a rich tobacco merchant. Finally, even this merchant turned against his adopted son, beat him with a cane, drove him out of the house, disinherited him, and refused to leave him a dollar in his will.

The story of Poe's marriage is one of the most beautiful tales in literature. He married his first cousin, Virginia Clem. He had no money at the time. He was twice as old as his young wife. He was twenty-six and she was thirteen. According to all the old copy-book adages, his marriage should have ended in swift and sure disaster.

But it didn't: It was a romantic success. Poe all but worshipped this child-wife of his, and his undying love for her inspired some of the most exquisite poetry that ever enriched the English language.

Edgar Allan Poe spun stories and created verses that were destined to be placed among the literary glories and treasures of the earth; and yet he couldn't sell these immortal masterpieces for enough to buy bread. For example, he gave the world a poem that has become immortal:

And the raven, never flitting, still is sitting, still is sitting
On the pallid bust of Pallas, just above my chamberdoor.
And his eyes have all the seeming of a demon that is dreaming,
And the lamplight o'er him streaming throws his shadow on the floor.

WRITER OF ALICE IN WONDERLAND

One day, about seventy years ago, a shy, timid, young man took three little girls out for a boat ride on the Thames River in England. When he stepped into the boat, this young man was unknown. But when he stepped out of it, three hours later, he was on his way to become one of the famous men of the nineteenth century.

His name was *Dodgson*. That is not the name you know him by; but that's his real name.

Sometimes he was called *Reverend* Dodgson and sometimes *Professor* Dodgson, for during the week, he taught mathematics in Oxford University, but on Sundays, he preached in a church.

When he tried to talk to grown-up people, he often became confused and stammered—but he always loved to tell nonsense stories to little girls. So, while out rowing his boat on the Thames River on this particular afternoon, he told a whimsical story to his three little companions.

He told them about a little girl who went to sleep and disappeared down a rabbit hole and awoke in Wonderland. They listened with wide-eyed astonishment, and forgot all about the boat ride and begged the professor to write the story for them; so he sat up all night doing it. and since one of the little girls had the name of Alice, he called the story *Alice in Wonderland.*

—Dale Carnegie, *Little Known Facts About Great Well Known People*

CATHERINE

Catherine the Great fell in love with an ugly giant, bearing the name of Potemkin. Potemkin had one eye. He had lost the other one in a tavern brawl.

Although Potemkin lived in a palace glittering with all the splendour and riches of Asia, he went about with nothing but house slippers on his bare feet. His hair was uncombed and he always needed a bath. He chewed his finger nails; and he ate raw onions and garlic. But Potemkin was a tornado of physical energy, and the mere touch of his hand filled Catherine with a vast and tender happiness. She called him her "golden pheasant," her "pigeon", her "bow-wow".

Her "bow-wow" was one of the greatest generals Russia ever had; and yet he was afraid of the noise of guns and trembled like a school girl whenever a cannon was fired.

Although Catherine was the richest woman in the world, she ate only two meals a day; and almost anyone in America of modest income enjoys better cooked food than Catherine the Great often had. She had her dinners served on plates of gold; yet if the cook burned the meat, she merely laughed and ate it just the same.

Although Catherine was one of greater voluptuaries that ever lived, she never drank wine nor an alcoholic liquor. But she did drink sweet currant juice, and she also drank five cups of strong coffee every morning. A whole pound of coffee was used to make those five cups.

—Dale Carnegie, *Little Facts About Well Known People*

CHARLIE CHAPLIN

Chaplin hasn't made a picture for two years; and besides, he is in business anyway, for he owns his own company.

No, this biggest money-maker is a man who never had very much education. He uses bad English. He wears old clothes, he is lazy, he is always late to an appointment, and he loves to chew gum. His name is *Will Rogers.*

He gets $375,000 a year for making three pictures; and he gets $400 a day or $2,800 a weak for his newspaper column. He gets a thousand dollars for merely making a funny speech. He gets $333 a minute for talking over the radio. Why, he can just pause between sentences and make ten or fifteen dollars.

He is fifty-four years old. He was born on Election Day and he has made half a million dollars cracking jokes about Congress, but he has never voted himself. Why?

Because he was in the show business for twenty-four years and never lived in one place long enough to register and vote; and he doesn't like to vote now because he wants to be able to speak his mind without any party prejudice.

Charlie Chaplin had a private secretary; and press agent for seven years. He travelled with him constantly; and yet his secretary, Carlyle Robinson, told me that, at the end of those seven years, Charlie Chaplin didn't know his last name.

COLUMBUS

It seems to me that we're all in the same boat with Christopher Columbus. He didn't know where he was going when he started. When he got there he didn't know where he was, and when he got back he didn't know where he had been.

—Dale Carnegie, *Little Known Facts about Well-known People*

On every 12th of October, we celebrate one of the most important events in our history, the discovery of America by Christopher Columbus; but here is a funny thing—Columbus did not discover America on October 12th. He discovered it on October 23rd. The calendar we are using now was originated by Pope Gregory. Columbus never heard of that calendar: it didn't even exist until one hundred years after he was dead. The American colonies adopted that calendar in 1752; and when we adopted it, we jumped time ahead exactly 11 days. Why? Because the calendar at that time was eleven days behind the sun. So, according to the present calendar, Columbus discovered America, not on October 12th, but on October 23rd.

— Dale Carnegie, *Little Known Facts about Well-known People*

THOMAS A. EDISON

Doctors looked at the shape of his head and predicted brain trouble.

Edison had a very poor memory—especially in his youth. In school, he forgot everything he was taught, and he was always at the foot of his class. He drove his teachers to despair. They declared that he was addle-brained, that he was too stupid to learn, and the doctors even predicted he would have brain trouble, for his head had an extraordinary shape. As a matter of fact, he attended school only three months during his entire life. After that, his mother taught him at home; and what a magnificent job she did, for he did all but transformed the world in which we live.

Yet, later in life, Thomas Edison developed a remarkable memory for scientific data, and he mastered most of the scientific facts in his vast private library. He developed an extraordinary ability to concentrate, to forget everything but the subject he had in hand.

One day, while he was deeply absorbed in trying to solve some scientific problem, he went to the court house to pay his taxes. He had to stand in line for some time; and when his turn came, he actually forgot his own name. One of his neighbours, seeing his embarrassment, reminded him that his name was

Thomas Edison. He afterwards declared that he couldn't have called his name for a few seconds then even if his life had depended upon it.

At one time he seriously thought of studying some system to improve his memory.

Edison frequently worked in his laboratory all night long. One morning, while he was waiting for his breakfast to be brought to him, he fell asleep. One of his assistants, who had just eaten some ham and eggs and was feeling in a jovial mood, wanted to fool the old man; so he placed his empty tray of dishes on the table in front of Edison. A few minutes later Edison awoke, rubbed his eyes, and looked down at the bread crusts and the empty plate and the empty coffee cup. He thought a moment and then came to the conclusion that he must have eaten breakfast before he had his nap; so he pushed back from the table, lighted a cigar, had a smoke, and started to work again and never knew the difference until his assistants broke into an uproar of laughter.

One evening when Thomas Edison came home from work, his wife said to him, "You've worked long enough without a rest. You must go on a vacation."

"But where on earth would I go?" asked Mr. Edison.

Just decide where you would rather be than anywhere else on earth," suggested the wife.

Mr. Edison hesitated. "Very well," he said finally, "I'll go tomorrow."

The next morning he was back at work in his laboratory.

—Dale Carnegie, *Little Known Facts About Great Men*

The story is told that when Western Union offered to buy the ticker invented by Thomas Edison, the great inventor was unable to name a price. Edison asked for a couple of days to consider it. Talking the matter over with his wife, she suggested he ask

$ 20,000, but this seemed exorbitant to Edison. At the appointed time, Edison returned to the Western Union office. He was asked to name his price. "How much?" asked the Western Union official. Edison tried to say $20,000, but lacked the courage, and just stood there speechless.

The official waited a moment, then broke the silence and said, "Well, how about $100,000?"

—J.M. Braude, *Wit and Humour*

H.G. WELLS

H.G. Wells was one of the highest paid authors on earth. He probably made a million dollars with his pen; yet he was brought up in pinching poverty.

The future author of *The Outline of History* started out in business life, at the age of thirteen, as a dry goods clerk. He had to get up at five o'clock, sweep out the store, build the fire, and slave for fourteen hours a day. It was drudgery, and he despised it. At the end of one month, the boss fired him because he was untidy and slovenly and troublesome.

Then he got a job clerking in a drug store. And again he was fired at the end of the first month.

He finally got a job clerking in another dry goods store. He had to eat, so this time, he held out a bit longer. But when the floorwalker wasn't looking, he would sneak down into the cellar and read Herbert Spencer.

Wells' mind was constantly blazing with ideas. He even got up in the middle of the night to put down stray thoughts in his notebook. And this lazy boy who was once fired because of incompetence as a dry goods clerk, said that he had enough material in his notebooks to keep him writing books for a hundred and fifty years.

He could write anywhere—in his London workshop, on the train, or under a beach umbrella by the seductive blue waters of the Mediterranean. He rented two villas on the French Riviera. One was a workshop, and the other was a guest house. He wrote all day and chatted with his guests only in the evening.

— Dale Carnegie, *Little Known Facts about Well-known People*

O. HENRY

O. Henry was famous short story writer who ever lived. More than six million copies of his books have been sold; and they have been translated into almost every language on earth.

O. Henry's life is a striking illustration of a man who battled against tremendous odds and succeeded, in spite of terrible handicaps.

First, he had the handicap of very little education. He didn't even attend high school; and he never saw the inside of a college; yet today his stories are studied as models of good writing in half the universities of the land.

Second, he was handicapped by the ravages of diseases. The doctors feared that he was going to die of consumption; so they took him away from his home in North Carolina, sent him down to Texas, and he got a job herding sheep on a ranch there.

Today, automobile tourists drive hundreds of miles out of their way to see that ranch; and as they approach it, they halt their cars and walk reverently over the ground where O. Henry once tended his flocks.

Third, he had the apparent misfortune of being thrown into prison.

Here he wrote lot of stories in loneliness.

—Dale Carnegie, *Little Known Facts about Well-known People*

JOSEPHINE AND NAPOLEON

Josephine wanted to meet Napoleon.

Josephine figured out a clever way to do it. She sent her young son, who was twelve years old, to ask Napoleon if he might have the sword of his (the boy's) dead father. Naturally, Napoleon said yes; and the next day Josephine powdered her nose and went to thank Napoleon, with tears in her eyes for his great kindness.

Napoleon was immensely impressed by Josephine's personality and by her extraordinary charm. He realized that she was above him, socially; so when she invited him to her house for tea, he was flattered. And when he came to tea, she told him he was going to be one of the greatest generals in all the history... Three months later, their engagement was announced.

Napoleon had a veritable passion for always being on time. His motto was "Time is everything," and he once said, "I may lose battles, but no one will ever see me lose minutes;" and yet he was two hours late for his own wedding! The Justice of the Peace who was waiting to marry them got so tired that he yawned and fell asleep before Napoleon arrived.

And the amazing part of it all is that, even on the battlefields, Napoleon found time to write Josephine a letter everyday. And what letters! Ardent, flaming, tempestuous affairs! In 1933, eight of Napoleon's love letters to Josephine were sold at public auction in London for £ 20,000.

- He decided to divorce her for one reason only: he wanted a wife who could bear him a son. It broke his heart to do it and he wept as he signed the divorce papers; and for three days after that, he sat in his palace, staring into space. Shortly after the divorce, Napoleon married Marie Louise, of Austria.

The curious part of it is that Marie Louise, like all Austrians had been brought up to despise Napoleon; and she prayed to Almighty God that she wouldn't have to marry him. But her father insisted that she did it for political reasons; and so she married him, by proxy, before she ever even saw him. But she didn't care for him; and when he began to lose battles, she deserted him, and even taught his own son to hate him.

Napoleon's first love and last love, and only real love, was Josephine. And after she died, he visited her grave and wept, saying,

"My darling Josephine, at least you would never have deserted me."

The last word that Napoleon ever spoke on this earth was the word "Josephine."

Spaceimen of a lovely letter written by Napoleon to Josephine:

> My dear Josephine
>
> You have inspired me with a love which has taken away my reason—I can't eat. I can't sleep. I can't care for my friends. I don't care for glory; I value victory only because it pleases you. If it weren't for that, I should leave the army and hurry back to Paris to fling myself at your feet.
>
> You have inspired me with a limitless love; you have filled me with an intoxicating frenzy. Never an hour passes without my looking at your portrait, and never an hour passes without my covering it with kisses.

LENIN

Lenin started in Russia the greatest economic experiment the world has ever known—an experiment that is bound to have some effect on you and me and almost everyone else in the world.

Lenin was a little, bald-headed, wrinkled man; and when he sat in a chair, his legs were so short that they hardly touched the floor.

He didn't care anything at all about his looks; his trousers were usually too long, his nose was slightly turned up, he had a squint in one eye and he probably never wore a silk hat or a frock coat in his life. He was happily married, and his wife loved him so much that she refused to leave him when he was exiled; so she went with him into exile in order to look after him and care for him.

He had a lot of spare time when he was an outcast in Siberia, so he became an expert chess player. He could play several games of chess at the same time; and he was so fascinated with chess that he used to play the game with his friends far away by mail.

As a child, Lenin was serious and gloomy, seldom played with other children and never took part in athletic games. When he grew to be a man, he had no interest whatever in music or poetry or religion; but he studied law and spoke four languages—French, German, Russian and English.

The Russian government hanged his brother because he was plotting to kill Czar Alexander the Third; and the Government later banished Lenin himself because of his radical opinions. They banished him to a small town in frigid Siberia. There Lenin saw, with his own eyes, the tragic poverty of the Russian peasants. They were so poor they could not afford to eat meat except on the great religious holidays—in other words, they ate meat about twenty times a year.

During the great famine of 1891, when millions of poverty-stricken peasants died of starvation, and typhus and cholera, Lenin became convinced that something radical had to be done. From that time on, he became a flaming revolutionist.

During the next twenty-five years, he was hounded and driven from one country to another, living at various times in Germany, Austria, France, Poland, Switzerland and England. When he lived in London, he would often go and sit for hours at a time beside the grave of Karl Marx, the father of Socialism.

Sometimes, in order to escape arrest, he went about disguised as a peasant, or sailor, or factory worker. Sometimes he wore false whiskers. Sometimes he masqueraded as a woman. He always, travelled with a false bottom in his trunk—and beneath the false bottom, he kept secret papers and incriminating documents. Sometimes he buried his secret documents in his vegetable garden and he planted onions and cabbage above them.

He wrote one of his revolutionary books in prison; and, in order to avoid detection, he wrote it in milk instead of ink. The writing could be read only after it was dipped in hot water. He taught his disciples to use invisible ink when they wrote to him. When he got one of these invisible letters, he would ask the prison guard for tea. Then, as soon as the guard's back was turned, he would dip the letter in the hot water and read it.

In November 1917, Lenin became dictator of Russia and confiscated all private property. The owners of the great estates fled in terror, as the peasants took possession. The peasants cut up rare and exquisite tapestries and made them into shoes. They took priceless vases, made by the master potters of Europe, and used them for pickle jars.

Russia was almost starving at the time and Lenin refused to take sugar in his tea because other people couldn't have sugar. Although he was the supreme ruler of Russia, he wouldn't permit himself to have even the simplest luxuries. He ruled Russia without having a staff of secretaries and he rarely dictated a letter. He worked from eighteen to twenty hours a day and wrote almost all his letters himself.

Five years later, he was suffering from hardening of the arteries, and he had a stroke of paralysis. He lost the power of speech, and he had to learn to talk all over again like a child. His right hand was paralyzed so he learned to write with his left hand. For two years, he fought desperately with death, saying over and over again, "There is so much work left for me to do."

Even that method of action was not fixed and unchangeable, but had to be suited to circumstances. That, at any rate, was

Lenin's view, and he justified it brilliantly by fitting his action to changing circumstances. He tells us that: "To attempt to answer 'yes' or 'no' to the question for the definite means of struggle, without examining in detail the concrete situation of a given moment at a given stage of its development, means to depart altogether from the Marxian ground." And again he said: "Nothing is final; we must always learn from circumstances."

—Dale Carnegie, *Little Known Facts about Well-known People*

ABRAHAM LINCOLN

Lincoln and his wife after marriage began to realize that they were exact opposites, in every way, and that they could never be happy. They were the exact opposites in temperament, in tastes, in training, and desires.

For example, Mary Todd had attended a snobbish finishing school in Kentucky; she spoke French with a Parisian accent, and was one of the best educated women in Illinois. But Lincoln had attended school a total of less than twelve months in his entire life.

She was extremely proud of her family. Her grandfathers and great grandfathers and great uncles had been generals and governors, and one had been Secretary of the Navy.

But Lincoln had no pride whatever in his family tree. He said that only one of his relatives had ever visited him while he lived in Springfield, and that one was accused of stealing a jew's-harp before he got out of town.

Mary Todd was deeply interested in dress and show and ostentation. But Lincoln took no interest whatever in his appearance. In fact, he would sometimes walk down the street with one trouser leg on the outside of his boot and the other trouser leg stuffed inside his boot.

Mary had been taught that good table manners were almost a sacred rite; but Lincoln had been reared in a log cabin with a dirt floor, and he stuck his own knife into the butter plate and did a score of things that shocked Mary and almost drove her wild.

She was proud and haughty. He was humble and democratic. She was intensely jealous; and created a scene if he merely looked at another woman. Her jealousy was so bitter and so unreasoning and so fantastic that it makes one gasp to read about it even now.

Lincoln then wrote the most pitiful letter of his life. It was written to his law partner who was then in Congress. This is the letter, word for word:

> I am now the most miserable man living. If what I feel were equally distributed to the whole human family, there would not be one cheerful face on earth. Whether I shall ever be any better, I cannot tell. I awfully forbode that I shall not. To remain as I am is impossible. I must die or be better, it seems to me.

We hear his aunt tell this story: One morning, Mr. and Mrs. Lincoln were having breakfast with the rest of the boarders, and Lincoln said something that displeased his wife; so she picked up a cup of hot coffee and dashed it into his face, and she did it in the presence of the other boarders. Lincoln didn't answer her. He didn't scold her. He said nothing, while the landlady brought a wet cloth and wiped off his face and his clothes. Similar incidents probably occurred in the Lincoln household for years.

But let us not judge Mrs. Lincoln too harshly. She finally went insane; and perhaps much earlier her mind was being affected by oncoming insanity.

One of the most beautiful things I know about Abraham Lincoln is the fact that he endured his unhappy home life for twenty-three years without bitterness, without resentment and without saying a word about it to anyone. He endured it with Christ-like forgiveness, and with a patience that was almost divine.

He could not save his family but he saved America from Partition through war and paid for it with his life.

When Abraham Lincoln wanted to memorize anything, he read it aloud so that he would impress it both on his sense of sight and his sense of hearing.

—J.M. Braude, *Wit and Humour*

One combatant who had been defeated in the decision and above whom the towering Lincoln stood head and shoulders, boastfully threatened Lincoln.

"See here, Lanky, I'll lick you!" he shouted.

Abe looked down comically at the small challenger. "All right," he said, "but let's fight fair. You are so small there isn't much of you for me to hit, but I am so big, you can't help hitting me. So you make a chalk-mark on me that will show just your size. When we fight, you must be sure to hit me inside this mark or it won't be fair."

The idea was so ridiculous, the little bully began to laugh, and the quarrel ended as a joke.

• Lincoln called in Ben Wade and Senator Daniel Voorhees to discuss the appointment of an Indian commissioner, explaining what kind of man he wanted to appoint.

"Gentlemen, for an Indian commissioner," said the President, "I want a pure-minded, moral, Christian man—frugal and self-sacrificing."

"I think," interrupted Voorhees, "that you won't find him."

"Why not?"

"Because, Mr. President, he was crucified about eighteen hundred years ago," said the senator.

—J.M. Braude, *Wit and Humour*

PT. MADAN MOHAN MALVIYA ON NIZAM OF HYDERABAD

He could buy and sell Rockefeller and Morgan, but he slept in a bed with no springs.

His name is Nizam Osman Ali Khan Bahadur Fateh Jung Asaf Jah; but he was usually called the Nizam of Hyderabad, and he is a descendant of the old Mogul Emperors who swept down through the Khyber Pass and looted India centuries ago. He ruled with a high hand over the richest state in India.

Well, for one thing, he had a harem filled with over five hundred women.

But he had one favourite and he rode around in a Rolls-Royce limousine, with the shades drawn, so that the unworthy populace could not gaze upon her royal face.

The richest man in the world got up every morning before dawn. But he did not have to jump out of bed and turn off the alarm clock, for His Exalted Highness was awakened from his dreams by a group of musicians who came into his presence playing and singing. Being a Mohammedan, he got up early so that he could spread out his prayer rug, turn his face towards Mecca, prostrate himself before Allah, and poured out his soul in prayer as the sun loomed over the hills of Hyderabad.

He had four servants whose sole duty in life was to dress him. Each servant dressed a different part of the royal body. One man, for example, was the trouser specialist. He would be insulted if you asked him to help put on the royal shirt. No sir, when he got on the Nizam's trousers he sat in the shade and rested up for the next morning's work.

The Nizam was an absolute monarch, with the power of life and death over fifteen million of his subjects and the common people flung themselves humbly upon the ground as he passed by.

Although he took a perfumed bath every morning, he did not use soap. He used the powdered bark of a tree instead. He did not have breakfast until four hours after he got up; and then he had a sort of combination breakfast and lunch. He did not drink tea or coffee—just milk or plain cold water.

He ate breakfast on plates of gold.

THE RICHEST MAN IN THE WORLD EATS SOUP WITH HIS FINGERS

The richest man in the world ate with his fingers. He did not use a knife, nor a fork, nor a spoon. He even drank his soup out of his fingers. His jaded palate is tempted by such rare dishes as curried peacocks and wild cranes and bird of paradise.

He usually wore a white silk coat, embroidered with gold, and had strings of pearls and diamonds looped about his neck; yet he had been seen in public, clad in a black tunic spotted with grease.

Although he had a barber, whose only duty in life was to keep him well groomed, he slipped occasionally and went about with his hair uncombed and his chin unshaved.

The Nizam of Hyderabad had chairs, couches, carriages, and even cannons, cast in solid gold and inlaid with emeralds and rubies. Of course, he could not shoot these golden cannons, because they were too soft, but they did make a mighty impression upon the visitor.

A lot of wealth came from the valley of Golconda, the richest diamond field in the world. From the incredibly rich Golconda mines had come the most celebrated jewels in the world—jewels such as the huge, gleaming Kohinoor, now worn by the Queen of England.

And in spite of all his incredible wealth, the Nizam liked to make a few dollars on the side, even as you and I. For example, he gave sumptuous banquets, and his invited guests were expected to bring a suitable present in cash. He sometimes had five hundred guests for dinner—and, at ten dollars a head, you could figure it out for yourself.

He went on regular shopping expeditions into the public market, tasting this food and that, and whenever His Exalted Highness admired anything, custom demanded that the shopkeeper gave it to him free of charge. So he went back to the palace with an army of servants carrying baskets of food didn't cost him a cent; and he sometimes sent these baskets to his friends with a price tag on each basket, specifying the amount that the friend must pay for the honour of receiving the gift.

Once, the Nizam announced that he was going to publish a book of his own poems. The ordinary copies were going to cost twenty dollars, and the royal copies were going to cost a hundred. Since none of the aristocracy of Hyderabad dared refuse to buy the songs of the Imperial Poet, the book sold like hot cakes in advance of publication. Years passed since then, but the royal poems had never been printed, and the money had never been returned.

The Nizam spoke perfect English, shot tigers from the back of an elephant, wore rings in his ears, gave his favourite wife two hundred dollars a month for spending money.

- Pt. Madan Mohan Malviya once came to the Nizam for contribution to install one university at Banaras but Nizam refused to give him anything.

Malviya came out on the road and followed the funeral procession of an old rich man. He started picking up the showered coins on the dead body. One of the courtiers saw it and ran to Nizam to tell him the fact. Nizam called Malviya and asked him why he was doing so. Malviya in his sarcastic way replied, "In Hyderabad living men don't give anything whereas dead men give generously."

Nizam felt ashamed and gave Malviya a cheque of handsome amount.

WALT DISNEY

To begin with, Walt Disney, the man who created Mickey Mouse and the Three Little Pigs, was almost unknown. Now, he is one of the most famous men in America and throughout the World.

The current edition of *Who's Who in Great Britain* lists Walt Disney among the great personalities of the world, and devotes more space to him than is given to the charming Prince of Wales.

Walt Disney was hard pressed to get enough to eat. Today, he is known and loved all the way from the tea fields of Sri Lanka to the fishing villages of the frozen North. Even the Eskimos, way up near the Arctic Circle, became so enthusiastic over the Mickey Mouse films that they saw in Juneau, Alaska, that they formed a Mickey Mouse Club which meets in an igloo.

At one time, Walt Disney was "broke". Today, he is very wealthy. He could swank about in a glittering Rolls Royce, if he wanted to; but instead, he uses an old car that he bought second-hand. He takes all of his profits and plows them back into his business. He says that making better pictures interests him far more than piling up millions.

Walt Disney believes the secret of success lies in being in love with your work. He says the idea of merely making money doesn't appeal to him. His work is the real thrill and adventure of his existence.

—Dale Carnegie, *Little Known Facts about Well-known People*

COLERIDGE

He read Arabian Nights and was obsessed with the tale of a man who was compelled to seek for a pure virgin. Whenever his mother was busy he would seize the book, carry it by the wall and read it. His father dismayed by the effect the book had produced on his son, burnt it.

—James Sutherland, *The Oxford Book of Literary Anecdotes,* p. 153

JOHN LAMB

John Lamb once knocked down Hazlitt, who was impertinent to him; and on those who were present interfering, and begging Hazlitt to shake hands and forgive him. Hazlitt said, 'Well, I don't care if I do. I am a metaphysician and do not mind a blow, nothing but an idea hurts me.'

—James Sutherland, *The Oxford Book of Literary Anecdotes,* p. 178

SIR ROBERT WALPOLE

When Sir Robert Walpole was dismissed from his employment, he retired to Houghton and walked into the library. When, pulling down a book and holding it some minutes to his eyes, he suddenly and sullenly exchanged it for another. He held that about one minute, and looking out a third returned it instantly to its shelf and burst into tears. "I have had a life of business so long" said he, "that I have lost my taste for reading, and now what shall I do?"

—James Sutherland, *The Oxford Book of Literary Anecdotes*, p. 62

P.B. SHELLEY

P.B. Shelley reading Plato about past life was pondering seriously to know what pre-existence was. While walking on Magdalen bridge, met a woman with a child in her arms. He asked her whether the child could speak and tell them about her past life. She replied he could not speak.

Shelley repeated his question and remarked the babe could speak if he willed for he was only a few weeks old. He could not have forgotten entirely experience of his pre-existence in so short a period. It was impossible.

—James Sutherland, *The Oxford Book of Literary Anecdotes*, p. 120

CHURCHILL

"It is impossible to obtain a conviction for sodomy from an English Jury. Half of them don't believe that it can physically be done, and the other half are doing it".

—Winston Churchill, *Delhi Times—What is hot*, 3-11-06, p. 22

MILTON

Some one asked Milton, "How many languages should girls learn?"

Milton replied, "A woman's one language is enough to torment a man, what will happen if she knows more than one language?"

- The renowned English poet Milton who was blind married a beautiful lady who was harsh-tempered.

A Friend of Milton who came to meet him told him, "Milton! You don't know how beautiful your wife is, as beautiful as rose".

Milton replied, "what you say is right. I cannot see the beauty of rose but I can feel the thorn which goes on pricking me day and night."

- One Indian Journalist went to England on tour. After looking about some places, he reached river Thames and stood on its bank.

One British journalist come near and asked him:

"Are you from India?"

"Yes"

"May I ask you one question?"

"Yes"

"Why is it that people of India have different colours, whereas we in Europe have the same colour?"

"Have you seen donkeys, they have the same colour, whereas horses have different colours?"

- Pakistani Minister, Feroze Khan Noon married third time and went to attend a meeting in which Sir Tej Bahadur was also present. Some persons from the meeting raised a question how to distinguish three wives of Sir Noon. Sir Sapru intervened and said, "the first wife be called Begum Noon, second one Mrs. Noon and the third one 'After Noon'.

—*Urdu Hind Samachar* 24-8-07 by,
Madan Gopal Nagina, Amritsar

- American President Truman was obsessed with word communism. He connected every bad incident with communist conspiracy. A delegation of film artists from India went on a friendly round of America. They requested the President to give them some time and their request accepted. A camera man came near them to have a photo of them along with the President.

As soon as he lighted the flash it burst. The President at once remarked, "it appears some communist has entered".

—*From Hind Samachar* by Nanak Chand,
Journalist Mukesion

WILLIAM THACKRAY

William Thackray tells of an Irish woman begging alms from him. When she saw him putting his hand in his pocket, the begger blessed, "May the blessing of God follow you all your Life". Thackray only pulled out his snuff box and no coin.

Immediately the beggar woman added, "And never overtake you!"

***

Chinese invasion was a disaster for India in 1962. At a Press Conference, Pt. Nehru, the Indian P.M. remarked in no uncertain terms, "we shall not give an inch of our territory to the Chinese". At this, a newspaper reporter asked Pt. Nehru, "Sir, just how many miles make an inch?"

***

Mr Chamberlain, the PM of England, was the guest of honour at a banquet, when coffee was being served the Mayor of the city who presided, leaned over to the PM and inquired, "shall we let them enjoy a little longer or had we better have your speech now?"

***

A young mother came to *Aristotle* and asked "when should I begin training my child?" Aristotle inquired, "How old is your child?". The mother replied that her son was five year old. Hearing this, Aristotle almost cried out, "Hurry home? You are five years late already."

A MISCELLANY

A Frenchman learning English said to his tutor, "English is a queer language, what does this sentence mean: Should Mr. Noble who sits for this constituency, consent to stand again, he will in all probability have a work over".

- Why does the Govt's revenue continue to be small despite high tax rates? This riddle confronted Frederick the Great of Prussia too. He got an answer for it at one of the state banquets he hosted.

An old general solved for Frederick in this manner: He took a lamp of ice and lifted it high for all to see, and then handed it to his neighbour and requested that it be passed on from hand to hand to the King. It was the size of a pea when it reached Frederick!

- G.K. Chesterton and Lord Beaverbrook were good friends. The latter owned a number of newspapers and periodicals.

After a sumptuous lunch the two men were walking down Fleet Street in London. Beaverbrook tapped the poet on the belly and asked: "Pregnant Chesterton?"

"No", replied the poet and added, "but I wish to God, you were!"

"Why"? demanded the Press baron

"It would stop your blasted periodicals".

- President Truman once remarked, "Any man who has the job I have, but doesn't have a sense of humour, won't last very long. Many Presidents since Truman show how the onerous burden of Presidency can be borne a little cheerfully with a smile. President Bill Clinton often surpassed professional comedians with his hilarious quips, jokes and asides. Talking about his visit to Jaipur, Bill Clinton told accompanying U.S. Journalists how the palace monkeys had snatched away his garlands and flowers and added "after the de-flowering they promptly lost all interest in me."

- Dr. Johnson was a fastidious stickler for the proper use of language. He was once assailed by a lady at a party with the words:

"Oh? Sir, you smell!" The good doctor quickly corrected her, "No, ma' am, you smell. I stink."

- While sitting at a table after dinner, George Washington complained that the fire burning him was very hot. A guest quipped, "But, Sir it behoves a general to stand fire!" "that's right", came the instant reply, "but it does not become a general to receive it from the rear".

- Gordan Brown the British P.M. during his visit to India, was conferred an honorary degree by the Delhi University. In his speech Mr. Brown pointed out that he was a lecturer at Glasgow University before he "descended into politics. Mr. Brown said a university stood for qualities like objectivity, rationality, impartiality and honest pursuit of truth. Immediately, thereafter he took a dig at politicians, a good number of whom was present among the audience, saying these were the qualities "that you have to leave behind when you go into politics."

- Field Marshal Manekshaw was a darling of his men. When the Naga rebels took a Gorkha soldier captive, Manekshaw rushed to the area, berated his subordinates, insisted on preparations to "take out" the village. Then some officer very politely but unofficially informed Manekshaw that the Gorkha soldier was actually philandering there. The "Capture" had been shown to cover up his absence. Messages went out and the soldier returned to face the consequences. Manekshaw only embraced the soldier and in a whisper querried, "was she worth it, son?"